# A History of

# Punishment
# and Torture

# A History of
# Punishment
# and Torture

CHANCELLOR
PRESS

ACKNOWLEDGEMENTS
Design: Darren Kirk
Picture research: Jenny Faithful and
Maxine McCaghy
Jacket design: Ben Barrett

First published in Great Britain
in 1996.
This 1999 edition published by
Chancellor Press,
an imprint of Bounty Books,
a division of the
Octopus Publishing Group Ltd,
2 4 Heron Quays, London,
E14 4JP.

Copyright © Octopus Publishing Group Ltd

ISBN 0-75370-236-3

A CIP catalogue record for this book
is available at the British Library

Produced by Toppan (HK) Ltd
Printed in China.

# INTRODUCTION

The study of punishment and torture through history is both macabre and mesmerising. In early times the authority of kings and noblemen was paramount and the penalty for criminal activity was death or serf-dom. From the Middle Ages until the 19th century the aims of punishment were deterrence and retribution. Consequently, the number of offences in Britain commanding the death penalty by the end of the 18th century amounted to more than 200. Little wonder that the criminal statutes were known collectively as 'The Bloody Code'.

In Europe the law required a confession to make a conviction. Eager volunteers manned the gruesome torture chambers where admissions from wrong doers were exacted. Appalling abuses took place in the name of king and country and the human toll rose hand-in-hand with the increasing population.

Public hostility towards the brutality of punishment grew. Barbaric torture was no longer tolerated by the masses nor was the death penalty for trifling offences. The twin punishments of transportation and incar-ceration came to the fore. Still, the plight of prisoners was hideous as they were regularly deprived of food, fresh water and fresh air.

As the 19th century wore on, enlightened thinkers, philanthropists and Christian reformers sought changes. At last the emphasis was on reforming prisoners instead of retribution. Mistakes were made with silent regimes and pointless labour which was aimed at making prison-ers reflect on their wrongdoing, but instead made many insane.

In the 20th century punishment has been dominated by incarceration and execution. Penologists have sought to establish penalties which are proportional to wrongdoing. In most countries, politicians and social reformers have been satisfied that a combination of the death penalty and imprisonment fulfils the key aims – reform of offenders, protection of society and deterrence of others.

**Above: When hard labour went out of fashion, prisoners were still expected to work for a living. Instead of productive jobs they were compelled to undertake fruitless tasks like pacing the treadmill, often in silence. The convicts worked in broody dissatisfaction – and sometimes went insane.**

**Right: The electric chair was first used more than 100 years ago and it is still in operation today.**

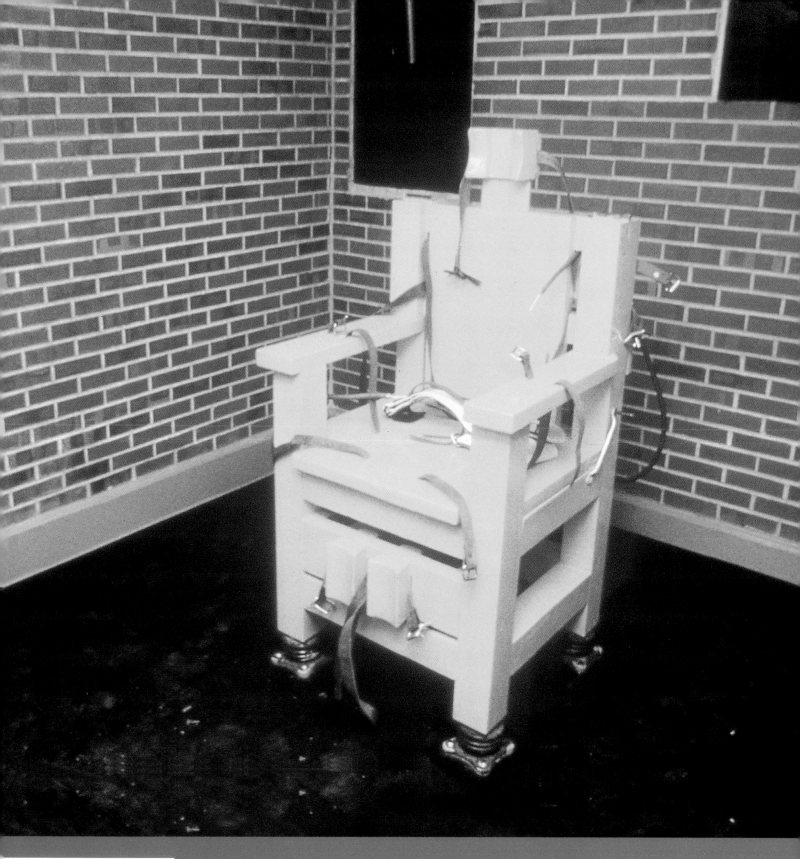

IN THE 20TH CENTURY PUNISHMENT HAS BEEN
DOMINATED BY INCARCERATION AND EXECUTION.
PENOLOGISTS HAVE SOUGHT TO ESTABLISH PENALTIES
WHICH ARE PROPORTIONAL TO WRONGDOING. THE
STUDY OF PUNISHMENT AND TORTURE THROUGH
HISTORY IS MESMERISING.

# PUNISHMENT
## WITHOUT MERCY

In the Dark Ages the thief and the murderer were as likely to suffer a death penalty as their 18th century counterparts. The loss of life had dual purpose, as punishment and as an offering to appease the gods. Alas for the victim, human sacrifice was frequently carried out in a hideously savage manner.

Even when Christianity spread across the globe there was little respite from the bloodshed. The Romans vied with their barbarian neighbours for new and agonising methods of death, creating a wealth of martyrs in the process.

# HUMAN SACRIFICE

## THE GODS DEMANDED A HEAVY TOLL FROM THEIR EARTHLY FOLLOWERS. HUMAN FODDER WAS NEEDED – AND WHO BETTER TO PAY THE ULTIMATE PRICE THAN FELONS AND THIEVES?

In the Dark Ages, the erring would find themselves sentenced to death by way of human sacrifice. At the time it was seen as the best hope of a good harvest and a cure for disease.

Every age had its own method of sacrifice. Given the evidence available today, it is difficult to assess whether all sacrifices were carried out as punishments or whether some died willingly, as messengers to the gods. It is equally hard to tell from excavated corpses whether mutilations took place before death by sacrifice, or after as part of a funeral rite.

The Celts had hundreds of gods to worship. Some were considered greater than others although only a few had specific purposes, for example, for war, fertility or cure. Caesar noted of the Celts: 'They believe that the execution of those who have been caught in the act of theft or robbery or some crime is more pleasing to the immortal gods but when the supply of such fails they resort to the execution even of the innocent.'

# LINDOW MAN

In 1984 a body dating back some 2,000 years was dug up in the peat bogs of Lindow Moss, near Manchester, England – complete with skin, hair and fingernails.

The body was so well-preserved by the peat that, at first, police suspected a murder victim had been found. They were right. Lindow Man, as he was known, was indeed murdered – scientists could tell by close examination that he was struck on the head several times with an axe and knocked unconscious. Presumably, this was to prevent him from suffering. Then a ligature was tied around his neck and twisted by means of a stick so that the victim was choked. The old-style garrotte was so effective that it broke his neck. His throat was then cut (although he was already dead) and the body was cast face down into the bog.

Lindow Man was certainly sacrificed as part of a ritual. Who can say if he was a criminal who suffered the ultimate penalty or if he volunteered?

A trace of poisonous mistletoe found in the deadman's stomach indicates that, before his violent ordeal began, he was subjected to the formalities of a last meal which was in some manner garnished with the plant. Mistletoe was frequently used by Druids for religious purposes.

**Police were onto the 'body in the bog' murder 2,000 years too late. Scientists found that the victim was killed after eating a last supper of poisonous mistletoe.**

---

Thanks to Strabo, the Greek writer and geographer who was alive at the same time as Christ, we know something of how those sacrificed were dispatched. '(The Celts) used to strike a human being whom they had devoted to death in the back with a sword and then divine from his death-struggle.' After gleaning clues to the future from the death throes the entrails would be examined for omens.

Alternatively, Celts might shoot victims with arrows or impale them at the chosen holy site. In common with other races, the Celts also burned their sacrifices. Humans were committed to the flames in a giant wicker cage in the form of a god. Dozens of young people might be crammed into such a colossus before a spark ignited the pyre. In attendance were the Druids, the highly organised priest and soothsayer network which inspired the Celts in France, Britain and Ireland at the time.

By Celtic rite, some women were sacrificed by immersion in water so that no blood was spilled. Alternatively, their breasts were cut off and put over their mouths before they were impaled to honour the goddess Adastra.

## THE UNDERWORLD CONNECTION

Celts were known to dig deep shafts, perhaps in a bid to communicate with the underworld. At the bottom of such shafts archaeologists have discovered human and animal bones.

There are Celtic shrines which have been unearthed to reveal quantities of human bones, again alongside the bones of animals and also tools which have been ritually smashed. The shrine at Gournay in France, dating from the 3rd century BC and in operation for about 200 years, was an enclosure surrounded by a ditch and a fence. The blood-

### THE STENCH OF ROTTING FLESH HELPED

### SAVE THE TREASURES OF CELTIC SHRINES.

stained altar is now long gone but inside there were pits containing gifts to the gods, with human, horse, sheep and pig bones, dotted at regular intervals between the skulls of cattle.

Gold was often left in abundance at such venues. No one dared to plunder the temples or shrines for fear of incurring the wrath of the gods. The odour of decaying flesh might also have kept potential thieves at bay!

Roman and Greek writers were genuinely appalled at the barbarity of the Celts and their religious practices even though their own cultures had bloody rituals.

# TIBERIUS AND CALIGULA

In the ancient world Rome was regarded as the capital of culture, philosophy and fine arts. During the days of the empire it also earned a reputation for excesses in sex and punishment. The embodiments of these practices were the emperors who, intoxicated by power, abandoned boundaries of decent human behaviour.

Tiberius became emperor in AD 14 at the age of 56. At first Tiberius seemed a model ruler, sometimes stern but always fair. This semblance of honour cloaked his debauched private life in which he had sex with women, men, boys and girls. He was also something of a sadist. If boys spoke out against the sodomy inflicted upon them he had their legs broken.

His closest advisor was Sejanus, a clever man who safeguarded his own position by undermining the status of others. Sejanus planted, in Tiberius' mind, the seeds of doubt about the loyalty of eminent figures of the day. A series of denunciations resulted in the deaths of entire families. In some cases children were compelled to kill their parents before being murdered themselves.

Bolstered by his success, Sejanus set-up the arrest and death of Tiberius' adopted son and likely successor, Germanicus. After his other son was poisoned, Tiberius was persuaded by Sejanus to move away from Rome and the advisor was Emperor of Rome in all but name.

Tiberius was probably insane by this stage – but lucid enough to spot the manoeuvrings of his lieutenant. From his hideaway he sent a letter condemning the activities of Sejanus to the Senate. On the day it was read aloud to the politicians Sejanus was carted off to jail and strangled. His body was dragged through the streets and left to rot. His skull was later taken to a public baths and used for ball games.

Characteristically, the bloodshed didn't end there. Livilla, mistress of Sejanus, was locked in a room by her own mother and starved to death. His children were slaughtered. The slightest whiff of treason was now enough to spark a wave of killing. A paranoid Tiberius ruled for another five years unchallenged.

## AN OUTWARD VENEER OF RESPECTABILITY MASKED THE VORACIOUS AND SORDID SEX LIFE IN WHICH TIBERIUS INDULGED.

**One day Sejanus ruled Rome, the next he was hauled away in disgrace to endure a terrible death.**

## KILLING JOKE

At dinner one day, Caligula burst into gales of laughter. When someone asked him what was so amusing he replied: 'It just struck me that I only have to give a signal and all your heads would be chopped off'.

## THE TYRANNY OF CALIGULA

If the kingship of Tiberius was cruel, there was worse to come. On his death Caligula, son of Germanicus, who was reared on persecution and violence, became emperor of Rome.

Most members of his immediate family were murdered or banished from the empire after incurring the wrath of Tiberius. In fact, special laws were passed to terrorise the descendants of Germanicus. During the early years of his reign, Caligula seemed a generous, warm leader who was welcomed after the dour Tiberius. The dark side of his nature inevitably emerged.

Among the first to feel the chill of his anger was the loyal adviser Macro. Although Caligula had been aided immeasurably by him during his ascent to power, he was now dismissed as '…the teacher of one who no longer needs to learn'. Caligula slept with his wife which, perversely, made Macro a pimp. Macro was killed on that charge.

Caligula's closest rival, Tiberius Gemellus, was put to death along with his entire family. In a bloody witch-hunt, he probed the papers of cases which had been brought against members of his family and had those involved slain without mercy.

Executioners were asked to make all killings a spectacle, as long and drawn out as possible. Caligula favoured a theatrical flourish to the death throes, having arms and legs chopped off or tongues hacked out before death. No one was safe from his macabre yearnings. Even lovers – drawn from both sexes – were left in no doubt as to their vulnerability. 'Off comes this beautiful head whenever I give the word,' he would coo.

Favourite among his lovers, however, were his three surviving sisters, particularly Drusilla. At her death, he mourned for months and made it a capital offence to laugh.

The opening of a bridge was marked by his lust for death. He pushed spectators into the river and told his men to drown them. Caligula was assassinated after four bloody years in power – an act widely celebrated.

## DEADLY POWER

Often there was no good reason for the blood-letting. Caligula decreed the cruellest punishments for sport. He might condemn his closest advisers and admirers and revel in the terror on their faces as they were hauled away. He described Rome as 'a city of necks waiting for me to chop them'.

# CRUCIFIXION

Few can be unfamiliar with the hideous punishment of crucifixion. It was a penalty devised by the Phoenicians, the people of a sea-faring and trading empire in Syria at its zenith in about 1,000 BC. Its prime trading point in Africa was Carthage.

The notion of death on a cross was imported from the Phoenicians by the Greeks, Assyrians, Egyptians, Persians and the Romans.

By the time Christ was crucified by the Romans it was considered the most humiliating form of death. Slaves and the worst criminals were candidates for crucifixion while Roman citizens were to a man spared its indignities, in favour of other less harrowing death penalties.

At first the crucifixion was carried out on a single stake. The victim was tied to it and left to die of thirst or starvation.

Then crosses were introduced, with either four arms, three arms or an X-style cross, sometimes known as a St Andrew's cross as he was reputedly crucified on one. While the details of different crucifixions might vary, in general the victim was first flogged and then forced to walk to the scene of the execution carrying the beam of the cross. The entire cross would have been too heavy for one person to bear.

**RUTHLESSLY SIMPLE, CRUCIFIXION WAS FIRST CARRIED OUT ON A SINGLE STAKE. THE VICTIM WAS SHACKLED TO IT AND LEFT TO DIE.**

## NAILED TO THE CROSS

Before being put on the cross the victim was stripped down to a loin cloth. He was then either nailed to the cross through his palms and the insteps of his feet, or tied by cord. His feet rested on a wedge of wood to prevent the weight of the body pulling the victim from the cross. The cross was then erected into a previously prepared fixing in the earth.

Sometimes the limbs of the crucified man were broken in order to hasten his death. His torment was enduring if his physical constitution was strong. There was the relentless sun beating on his unprotected skin, the flies feasting on his sweat and often a choking desert dust in the air. Compassionate judges ordered that the men be put out of their misery if they had not died by sundown.

Usually, crucifixions were carried out in batches, so six or seven crosses might appear in one spot. Much as the gibbet was used later on, victims were left on the cross as an example. Afterwards, the cross was customarily buried with the victims.

**Intolerably painful, unconciousness on the reversed cross occurred quickly. Death by crucifixion was otherwise horribly slow.**

# JAPANESE CRUCIFIXION

In Japan the agonies of crucifixion were refined. The executioner armed himself with light spears and spent a leisurely hour needling them into the body. Only if the bribe was sufficiently attractive would the spear penetrate the heart. Otherwise, the tormentor prided himself on narrowly missing all the vital organs and so keeping his victim alive. That method was used until the 19th century.

Some refinements emerged during the history of crucifixion. The victim might be attached upside-down to the cross. While this might appear even more callous it in fact was a blessing as the sufferer swiftly lapsed into a state of unconsciousness.

Happily, crucifixion was abolished by the Roman emperor Constantine in the 4th century AD. It was still used in France, however, until at least 1127 when Louis the Bulky insisted that Bertholde, the killer of Charles the Righteous, be crucified. Jews and heretics were amongst those most likely to find themselves on French crosses.

**The cross of St Andrew was so called after the disciple and patron saint of Scotland was martyred upon it.**

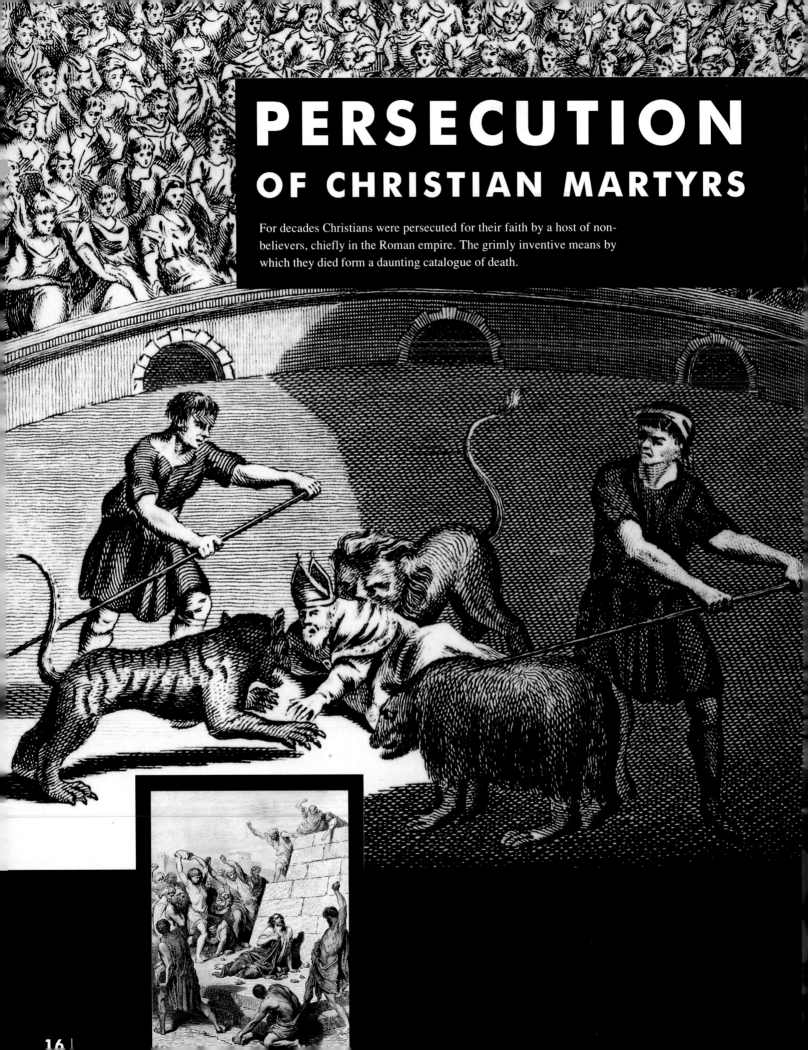

# PERSECUTION
## OF CHRISTIAN MARTYRS

For decades Christians were persecuted for their faith by a host of non-believers, chiefly in the Roman empire. The grimly inventive means by which they died form a daunting catalogue of death.

# FIRE

Fire power was used time and again to torment and torture. The agony might begin when prisoners gripping incense were forced to put their hands in hot coals. As a preliminary, others were compelled to walk across burning coals – in the knowledge that worse was to come.

Some were cast into pits lined with hot coals. Others met their end in a cauldron of boiling oil or molten lead. Martyrs were burned alive inside casks, tied with ropes drenched in oil which would burn into the flesh when they were lit by a spark. Or they had their limbs pegged to the ground so they were spread-eagled over hot coals.

Martyrs were immobilised in a suit of iron and then shod like horses with red-hot shoes which would strip the flesh from their feet. Equally painful was the iron helmet, glowing with heat, which was forced onto their heads.

Large human frying pans were fashioned by blacksmiths to cook the Christians slowly to death. There were also iron beds, to which they were bound, with fires lit beneath. Once again, the victims were broiled alive.

Apart from crucifixion, Christians were hung upside-down by one or both feet or hung by one or both arms with weights tied to their ankles. Women were occasionally hung by the hair. While they were hanging the unluckiest were also scorched with a flaming torch.

Eager executioners were ready to dispatch Christians, by beating them with cudgels or stoning them. Some chose to kill their victims by crushing them under heavy stones while others preferred to use a specially made press.

Amputation was among the options open to executioners. Some went so far as to cut the victims in two. Executioners inflicted mortal injuries with stakes, arrows, axes and spears.

Some martyrs were thrown from cliffs, perhaps helplessly bound to the circumference of a wooden wheel beforehand. Instead of on rocks or in the sea, some met their fate after being tossed into a lime kiln.

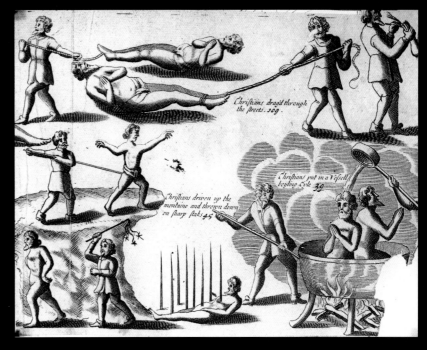

**A miserable fate awaited Christians who refused to deny their faith. They were dragged through the streets, flogged, tossed from mountain tops, impaled on stakes and boiled in oil.**

## COCKS AND VIPERS

If the Christian was to be killed without bloodshed he might be shut in a lead box and drowned in a river. There was a custom which persisted into the Middle Ages to put the condemned man in a sealed bag with a cock, a viper, a dog and an ape. The bag and its contents would then be thrown into deep water.

Stories of Christians being thrown as fodder for wild animals are well documented. Sometimes the victim was wrapped in hide to further excite the animals, which might include dogs, lions or bulls.

Even among this appalling variety, some methods appeared markedly more sadistic than the rest. There were cases of men with their hands tied behind their backs being hoisted up by the wrists and dropped on to a bed of spikes.

Pinioned martyrs might be smeared with honey to attract a swarm of bees. Consequently, they would be stung to death.

If there were two mature saplings in the vicinity, the trees were pulled down to ground level and the victim tied upside-down to them. The curled branches were then released like springs, violently ripping the body in different directions. All these grievous punishments were recorded in 16th century Papal papers although the abominations took place centuries earlier.

# THE FALL OF ROME

Nero is remembered as the Roman Emperor who 'fiddled while Rome burned'. The tyrannical madman played the lyre as he surveyed a blaze which raged for six days and destroyed much of the city.

By some bizarre logic, he blamed the Christians for the great fire (although he is suspected of being the firebug) and sought revenge. Christians were fed to packs of ravenous dogs by the dozen. He favoured crucifixion and, most galling of all, he had Christians doused in boiling pitch and then set alight providing human torches to light his route home.

To most people the word slavery conjures up visions of the black slaves shipped from Africa, and latterly the Caribbean, to the American south.

Yet slavery has existed throughout history with the earliest records of the Shang dynasty in China in the 18th century BC indicating the extensive use of slave labour.

At the time of Christ, an estimated five per cent of the Chinese population was enslaved.

**PROSPECTS FOR SLAVES IN ANCIENT TIMES WERE NOT GOOD. THE EGYPTIANS KILLED THEM BY THE SCORE OFTEN SO THAT THEY COULD SERVE THEIR OWNERS IN THE AFTERLIFE.**

In China debtors could sell wives and children into slavery to satisfy their creditors. The relatives of executed criminals could also find themselves enslaved.

Slaves were not only created by a more powerful nation rounding up the citizens of another. Slavery was frequently used as a punishment for debtors and minor criminals as well as prisoners of war.

The Greeks, Koreans, Hindus, Native Americans, Romans, Vikings, Africans and Turks were among the prominent cultures to employ slaves. In England in 1086 the Domesday book records that ten per cent of the population were enslaved. In some areas the figure was as high as 20 per cent.

Prospects for slaves in ancient times were not good. The Egyptians killed them by the score often so that they could serve their owners in the afterlife. Evidence of this kind of sacrifice was found in the Egyptian pyramids.

The natives of America sought advancement through celebrations known as potlatches. As a gesture of their wealth the Yurok Indians, who lived on the coast, were known to sacrifice their slaves on these high occasions. Other tribes also murdered slaves who had become old or unwanted, tossing their bodies into the sea.

It is believed many ancient societies bought slaves with the sole intention of sacrificing them. Elders in the ruling bodies would then eat the flesh. Much later the fate of slaves was equally precarious. Roman law decreed that if a slave killed his owner, all the other slaves under the same roof should be communally put to death.

While slaves existed, so too did a slave trade, captives being shipped around the globe to be bought and sold. It was in the interests of the ship's captain to keep his human cargo healthy, but there were intolerable hardships to suffer on board, including disease and shortages of food and fresh water.

Some enlightened societies allowed slaves to buy their freedom with relative ease. This was likely to be the case if there was no pressing labour shortage.

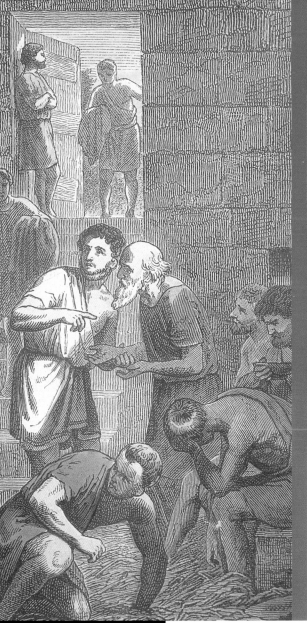

## SPARTACUS

Revolts by slaves were rare and the first signs of an insurrection were ruthlessly crushed. One of the best known was that by Spartacus, a gladiator in the Roman empire who was as bonded to his masters in the same way as slaves. In 73 BC he gathered an army which inflicted five defeats on the Romans before being beaten in a battle against Marcus Licinius Crassus. The rebels were hanged or crucified, with gibbets and crosses lining the roads from Rome.

**RUNAWAYS WOULD BE SMEARED WITH SWEET MOLASSES AND THEN TIED DOWN AS FOOD FOR ANTS. SO VORACIOUS WERE THE INSECTS THAT THEY WOULD STRIP THE FLESH FROM THE BODIES.**

## THE RIGHTS OF ANCIENT SLAVES

The Hebrews and later the Romans and the Greeks changed the status of a slave by law, from a thing to a person. Thereafter, anyone who killed his slave by torture, poison or fire faced the death penalty. Ch'ing Chinese law also punished the slave-owner who killed his chattel, the punishment all the more harsh if the dead man had done no wrong.

While sexual relations between master and female slave were generally accepted (even if the female was raped) an affair between a mistress and a slave was doomed. The Greeks and the Romans put the slave to death. Byzantine law had the slave burned alive and the mistress executed for her part in the affair. A white woman who fraternised with male blacks on the Danish Virgin Islands in the 18th century was fined, imprisoned and then deported.

In any society, ancient or modern, a slave who killed or otherwise broke the law could expect the heaviest punishment. The response of the French rulers of Haiti to rebel slaves in the 18th century provides a gory example.

Runaways would be smeared with sweet molasses and then tied down as food for swarms of ants. So voracious were the insects that they would strip the flesh from the bodies of the unfortunate slaves. The French were also known to put gunpowder up the backsides of erring slaves and set it alight. Sometimes slaves were hung from trees by nails which were driven through their ears. The 'justice' was gruesome.

Europe's most enslaved race were the Slavs who were taken to Russia, Germany and across the whole continent.

As early as the 1500s the slave trade was condemned as immoral and counterproductive by French thinker Jean Bodin. He was centuries ahead of his time. It was a further 200 years before the anti-slavery lobby gained the power and credibility to bring about change.

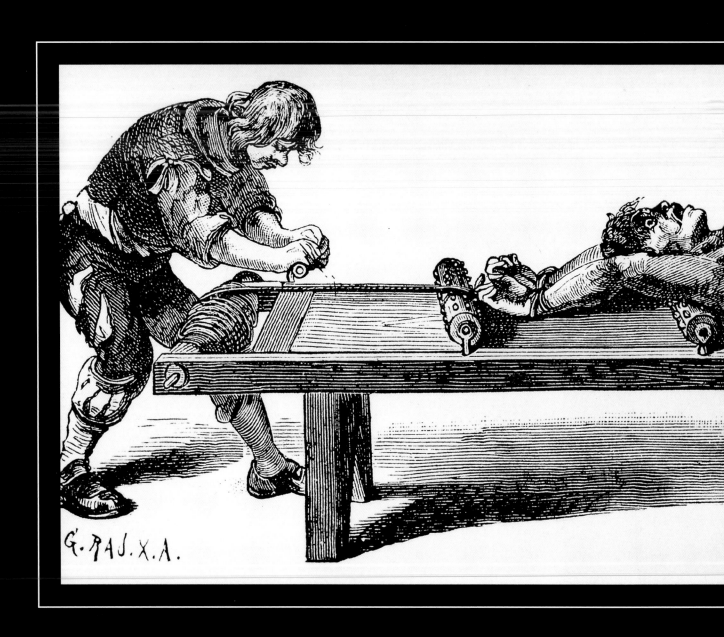

# MEDIEVAL JUSTICE

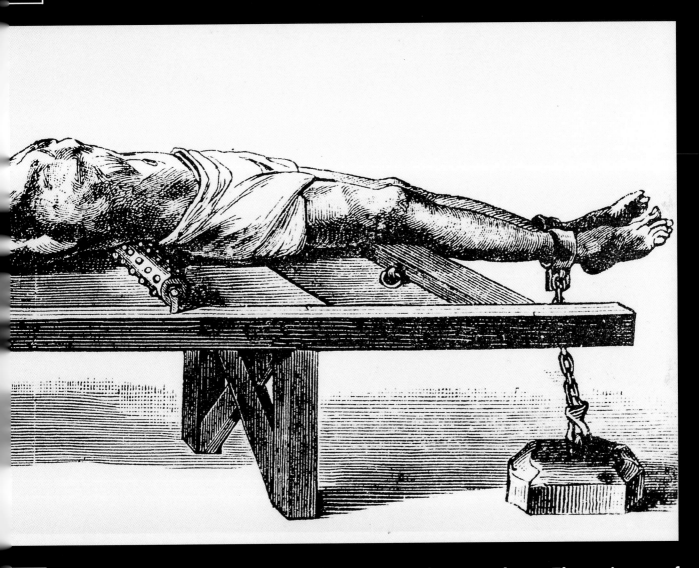

Life was cheap, human suffering worth even less. The misery of medieval Europe lay in its barbaric death penalties and its appalling torture chambers. The agonised screams which rang out as victims were being tormented in the name of the law meant nothing to the black-hearted agents of prince, Pope or government. Confession was the aim of the game – no matter what it cost.

# ORDEAL BY FIRE OR WATER

## A JUST AND RIGHTEOUS GOD WOULD INTERVENE TO PROTECT THE INNOCENT . . . WOULDN'T HE?

A dilemma confronted the elders of medieval society: just how could they discern who was guilty when so much was dependent on the word of the accused?

Various methods of proving innocence or guilt evolved, some more effective than others. Among the most notorious were trials by ordeal – either fire or water. From ancient times people believed that a man would be immune to the effects of the flames if he was innocent, receiving protection from the gods. The same notion was accepted in the Middle Ages in Christian Britain. Before the ordeal began there was a religious rite lasting for three days in which the accused underwent fasting, prayers, the taking of sacraments, exorcism and blessings. Then it was time to be exposed to the fire. Sometimes that meant carrying a

### HOT COALS, SMOULDERING IRON OR COLD WATER WOULD LEAVE THE INNOCENT MAN UNSCATHED.

lump of hot iron for a set distance, something in the order of three yards (three metres). For petty offences the lump of iron weighed about a pound (450 grams) but for more serious charges it could be as much as three pounds (1.5 kilos).

Alternatively, the ordeal could involve walking blindfolded over hot coals. Following the ordeal the wound caused by the flames was bound up. Three days later came an inspection of the skin to divine guilt or innocence. The man with an open sore was guilty, those who had healed were not. It is fair to say that the outcome of this ordeal would have been loaded against the accused, had it not been for the power of bribes and the corruption of the officiating clerics. For a fee the irons and the coals would be sufficiently cool to tolerate.

## WATER TORTURE

Likewise, the ordeal by boiling water was unlikely to prove innocence unless cash or valuables changed hands. The water in this case represented the flood of the Old Testament, from which only the righteous few escaped. Again, a three-day religious rite was carried out prior to the ordeal. Afterwards, if the ordeal was carried out by the book, the accused faced plunging their hand into boiling water, to the depth of the wrist. More serious offences demanded that the arm was submerged up to the elbow. The scald was bound up for three days before examination.

Ordeal by cold water involved the accused being tied at hands and feet and being lowered into water by a rope that was attached around his waist. There was a knot in the rope a specified distance from the body. If both body and knot went beneath the surface of the water it proved innocence. Should the knot stay dry the man was proven guilty.

It was common knowledge that the results of ordeals could be fixed and ultimately the process was so devalued that the Papal authorities banned the practice in 1215. The ban was slowly enforced throughout Europe in the 13th century.

## TRIAL BY COMBAT

Trial by combat also relied on the intervention of God to ensure that justice was done and the guilty punished. The duel might be fought on foot or on horseback with a choice of weapons which in Britain were paid for by the state. Inevitably, such battles drew crowds who would support one protagonist above the next.

The principle that might was right occasionally left the church with some explaining to do. For example, in 1100 a merchant who accused a monk of stealing sacred cups from a church was beaten in just such a duel.

Later the same monk – through the ordeal of water – was found guilty of

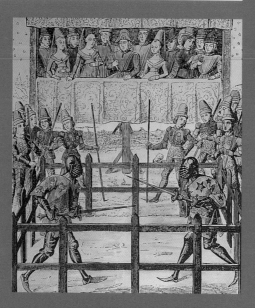

**The outcome of a trial by combat was seen as an indisputable verdict of guilt or innocence. In reality, only luck had the innocent man coming out on top. It was a far cry from justice.**

**Churchmen and onlookers alike had unshakeable faith that God would ensure justice was done.**

another offence and confessed to the first. Clearly the merchant, who was right, had not after all been protected by God. Quick-thinking churchmen lay the blame at the door of the hapless merchant by proving he had promised the monk not to say a word about the theft and was punished for breaking that pledge.

The accused were permitted to appoint a champion to fight on their behalf. Despite the illustrious title, freelance champions were invariably from the lower orders of society and commanded little respect. The practice of trial by combat disappeared across Europe from the end of the 14th century.

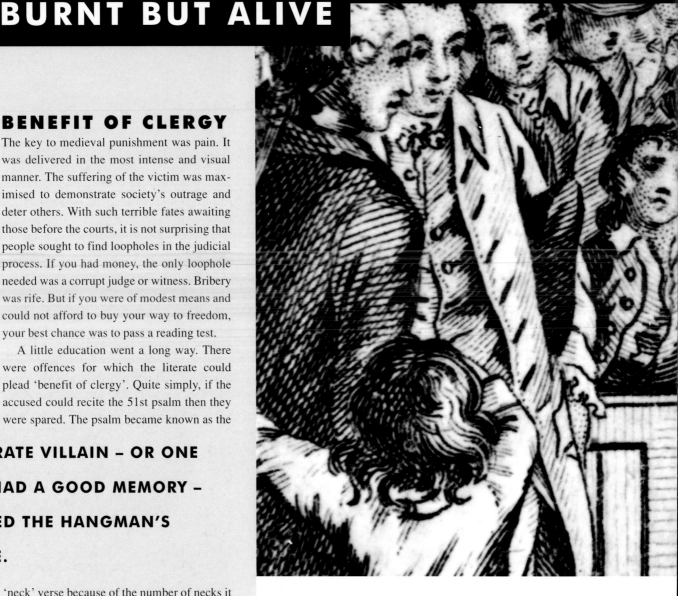

## BENEFIT OF CLERGY

The key to medieval punishment was pain. It was delivered in the most intense and visual manner. The suffering of the victim was max-imised to demonstrate society's outrage and deter others. With such terrible fates awaiting those before the courts, it is not surprising that people sought to find loopholes in the judicial process. If you had money, the only loophole needed was a corrupt judge or witness. Bribery was rife. But if you were of modest means and could not afford to buy your way to freedom, your best chance was to pass a reading test.

A little education went a long way. There were offences for which the literate could plead 'benefit of clergy'. Quite simply, if the accused could recite the 51st psalm then they were spared. The psalm became known as the

**A LITERATE VILLAIN – OR ONE WHO HAD A GOOD MEMORY – ESCAPED THE HANGMAN'S NOOSE.**

'neck' verse because of the number of necks it had saved. A brand laid discreetly against the fatty part of the thumb ensured that no one could plead 'the clergy' twice.

Benefit of clergy emerged as a wrinkle in the law because clerics in the Middle Ages were subject to both secular and ecclesiastical codes. So the clergy were made exempt from secular rulings and were punished by the church alone. At the time clerics were the only sector of society likely to be able to read and write. The sight reading test seemed an ideal way of sorting friar from thief.

However, as education gradually spread among the populace the test became obsolete. Smart villains would learn the psalm off by heart and recite it word for word with a book in front of them – yet remain unable to read.

As the years went by benefit of clergy was outlawed in successive statutes. But it wasn't until 1706 that the literacy test was finally halted by law.

## BRANDING

Branding was popularly used in Europe in the Middle Ages but by then it had been in use for thousands of years elsewhere. Babylon law, in force some 4,000 years before Christ, included branding. It was employed as a penalty for those who slandered married women or priestesses. The Greeks, the Romans and the Normans had all used branding, too.

In medieval times the brand, applied to the face or body, revealed the crime for which the victim had been convicted. The letter 'R' denoted a robber, 'B' was the sign of a blasphemer, 'S' indicated a slave, 'SL' stood for seditious libeller and 'F' for fray-maker – those guilty of causing a disturbance in church.

A law passed in the reign of Edward VI (1547–53) permitted vagrants and vagabonds to be marked with the letter 'V'. Cruelly, the same law allowed whoever brought the vagrant to court keep them as a slave for two years. This harsh Act was repealed in 1636.

Perhaps one of the most painful brands was that scored into the tongue. Quaker preacher James Naylor was punished for making himself the object of worship among people in Bristol in 1656. He was pilloried, whipped, had his tongue holed by a hot iron and was subsequently sentenced to imprisonment with hard labour.

**Above: A petty criminal was marked for life after a courtroom branding – the mark made it hard to get work and often led to a life of crime.**

**Left: Edward VI succeeded to the throne when he was nine years old. Even at that young age he was a Protestant zealot and revealed traits of barbarous cruelty before his death at 16.**

After a victim had been branded he was easily identifiable. This was important in an age where it was difficult if not impossible to verify the identity of anyone.

The brand, administered with a red-hot iron, also forewarned the felon's neighbours of a potential criminal tendency which the authorities believed was a good thing. Their glee was ill-founded, however, for after branding, a man was generally unemployable and was compelled to lead a life of crime.

It was the executioner's job to carry out brandings in open court. After the deed, he would look up to the judge, inquiring: 'A fair mark, my lord?' If the answer was no, the branding was repeated.

By the 14th century this was on the wane in England where it was replaced by hanging for major offences and the pillory or flogging for minor ones. Branding was outlawed in Britain in 1779.

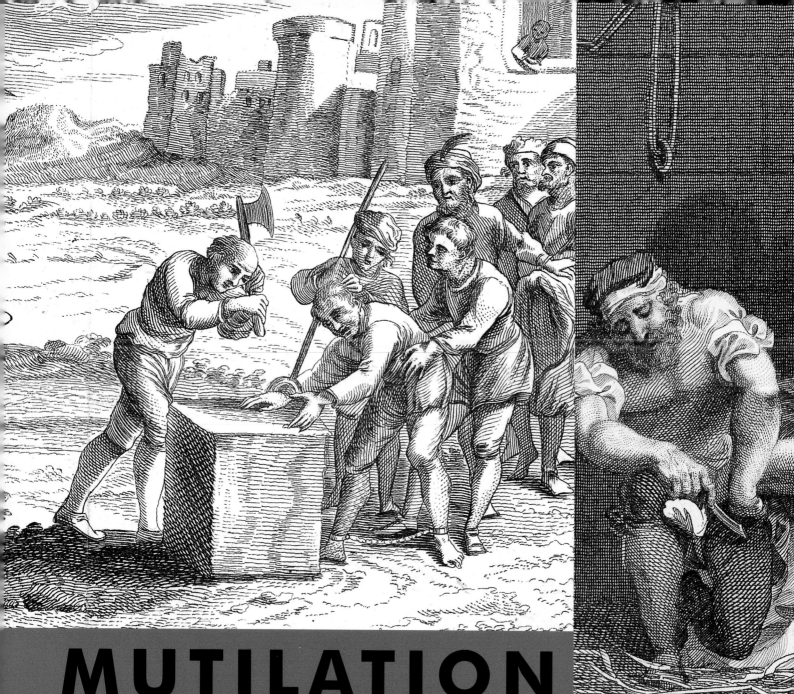

# MUTILATION

**IN THE MIDDLE AGES THE SWING OF AN AXE DELIVERED JUSTICE TO THE ERRING. THE LUCKY ONES LIVED TO SEE ANOTHER DAY – MINUS A LIMB.**

A thieving hand was abhorred by courts and citizens of medieval times and their remedy was short, sharp and to the point. The offending limb was cut off.

As the Middle Ages progressed the popularity of mutilation peaked and then fell. It was tempting for the law-givers of the day to make the punishment fit the crime. Therefore, a thief would lose his hand or perhaps his covetous eyes. A poacher would risk his legs, by which he trespassed on another's land.

Yet there is a record of money-lenders in Britain in 1124 having their right hands – and their testicles – cut off by order of King Henry I. With the same sadism, a woman in Portsmouth had her breasts severed.

Frequently, mutilation occurred while the victim was incapacitated in the pillory. As his head and hands were secured in the wooden framework, it gave the law enforcer ample opportunity to slit his nose or tear off his lip. Often, the penalty would be the loss of one or both ears. As a precursor, the ear might be nailed to the woodwork of the pillory.

In the cruellest of cases the victim whose ears were pinned firmly to the pillory was left to wrench his head away in order to secure his freedom. Habitual felons lost first one ear, then the next. Afterwards, the stump of the ear was shaved down.

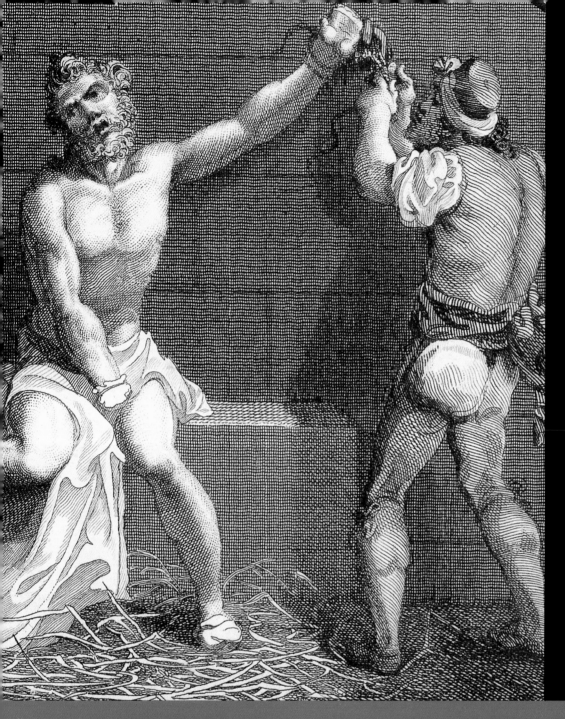

## HUNG, DRAWN AND QUARTERED

The mutilation of the dead also occurred. It became the custom to punish the most reviled criminals, those who were convicted as traitors, by hanging, drawing and quartering them. The drawing was the method by which they arrived at the gallows. They were affixed to hurdles and pulled by a horse. After being hanged their bodies were taken down, beheaded and cut into four quarters. Just as severed heads were set upon poles and placed at vantage points, so were the quarters.

William the Conqueror was a keen exponent of mutilation as was one of his heirs, Henry II. Robbery, murder and arson were among the crimes that could result in a penalty of amputation of the right hand and right foot.

In England during the 13th century, thieves might lose a thumb if found guilty of petty theft. The penalty for not attending church in the time of King Henry VIII was the loss of one or both ears. Anyone striking a blow in a palace or the court of King Harry was liable to lose their right hand.

His son and successor, Edward VI, introduced an Act by which the crime of brawling in a church or churchyard was punishable by mutilation. The church threw in excommunication for good measure.

For seditious libel in the reign of Elizabeth the perpetrator's hand was severed by a

**Torturers cut off the fingers and toes of a 15th century prisoner in his dungeon.**

cleaver. At this point, mutilation had all but died out and its reintroduction caused something of a sensation.

A witness saw the writer Stubbs deprived of his hand and wrote: 'When his right hand was struck off, he plucked off his hat with his left hand, and said with a loud voice: "God save the Queen." The multitude standing about was deeply silent, either out of horror at this new form of punishment or out of commiseration with the man'.

Poor standards of hygiene and medical science meant that the punishment of mutilation was tantamount to a death penalty for many. Treatment of open wounds was primitive and deadly infections were commonplace.

# TORTURE
## CHAMBERS

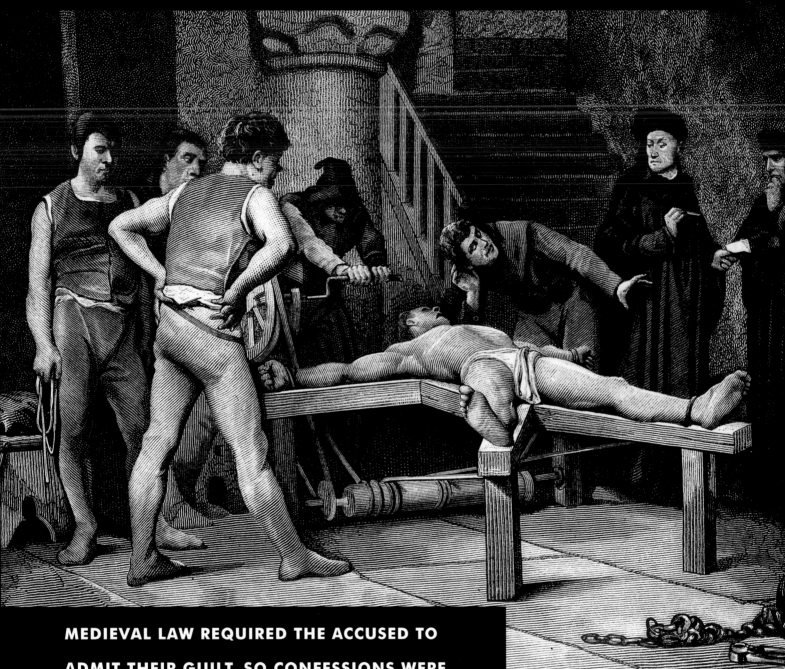

**MEDIEVAL LAW REQUIRED THE ACCUSED TO ADMIT THEIR GUILT. SO CONFESSIONS WERE EXTRACTED AT ANY PRICE. NO MATTER THAT THE 'GUILTY' PLEA WAS WON BY COERCION OF THE VILEST MEANS.**

With ingenuity and growing expertise, torturers in medieval times inflicted pain which was breathtakingly acute.

At their disposal was a range of implements designed with one purpose, to cause agony. Consider the 'Iron Maiden of Nuremberg', a device calculated to wring the

## PLEAD OR PAIN

Torture was never legalised in Britain. However, the law-makers saw little harm in prisoners undergoing physical torment to make them plead, guilty or not guilty. Frederick the Great abolished torture in Russia in 1742. In France torture was used as a means to extract confessions until the revolution in 1792 when it was scrapped.

**THUMBSCREWS WERE ANOTHER POPULAR DEVICE AMONGST TORTURERS – THEIR EFFECTS COULD BE DEVASTATING AND THEY WERE MERCILESSLY EMPLOYED FOR CENTURIES.**

most hideous suffering from the poor wretch confined in it. The maiden was a tomb-sized container with folding doors. Upon the inside of the doors were vicious spikes. As the prisoner was shut inside he would be pierced along the length of his body. The talons were not designed to kill outright, however, and the pinioned prisoner was left to slowly perish in the utmost pain.

In his quest to gain a confession, the torturer could also call upon the rack to terrorise his suspect. The victim was tied to a board by his wrist and ankles. Two rollers at each end were then turned – pulling the body in opposite directions often until it broke. Thumbscrews were another popular device amongst torturers – their effects could be devastating and they were mercilessly employed for centuries.

In medieval Europe, the fate of a man who confessed to a crime under torture was unlikely to be any less gruesome than if he were to allow the torturer to finish his painful work. With a firm belief in the power of a visual deterrent, European rulers were likely to hang criminals publicly by their thumbs or wrists. Cruelly, they favoured a barbaric penalty for poaching. The unlucky hunter would have hot lead poured into his ear. Barons could also administer a flogging, a fine, hard labour or a spell in the local stocks for the non-payment of rents.

## A TORTUROUS END

It was the era when people were buried alive although the punishment was not common. In the hope of eternal youth, Erzcebet Bathory, a niece of the King of Poland murdered more than 600 women so she could bathe in their blood. She was walled up alive for her outrageous crimes. Little wonder that many men died in the torturer's chamber rather than at the hand of the executioner.

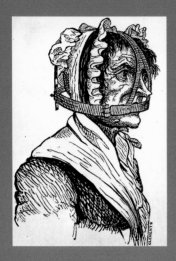

Nags were hags and suffered accordingly. Women's punishments were calculatingly cruel and often dangerous.

# PUNISHMENT OF
# WOMEN

## A READY WIT AND AN ACID TONGUE WERE ONCE PUNISHABLE OFFENCES FOR THE FAIRER SEX.

For women there were punishments designed to humiliate as well as to hurt. The scold's bridle took many appearances but in essence each was the same – a metal cage to clamp around the head with a built-in gag. Included in the design of some was a bell which rang when the 'scold' was paraded around the town. Of course, in the streets she was subjected to the jeers of the crowd. In Ipswich the scold was drawn around the town on a cart in the 'gagging' chair or 'Tewe', as it was known. The bridle, also known as the brank, was first used at the end of the Middle Ages in Scotland. It was rarely used after the start of the 19th century.

A scold was defined as: 'A troublesome and angry woman who by brawling and wrangling amongst her neighbours breaks the public peace, increases discord and becomes a public nuisance to the neighbourhood.' It remains unclear why men should not be pulled up on a similar charge. It was up to the judges to pronounce on whether a woman was indeed a scold. Frequently, it was a disgruntled husband bringing his wife to court.

The town jailer kept the bridle and was on call to apply it. In 1858 William Andrews gave a talk before the Architectural, Archaeological and Historic Society of Chester which gave further clues to its use.

'In the old-fashioned, half-timbered houses in the borough, there was generally fixed on one side of the large open fireplaces a hook so that when a man's wife indulged her scolding propensities, the husband sent for the town gaoler to bring the bridle and had her bridled and chained to the hook until she promised to behave herself better for the future.' This was presumably carried out as a favour to the husband, to spare him the trouble of appearing in court.

The first bridles were seen in Edinburgh in 1567 and in Glasgow, from 1574. By 1632 there was one as far south as Surrey. It was donated by a man called Chester and inscribed: 'Chester presentes Walton with a bridle, To curb women's tongues that talk too idle.'

## DUCKING STOOL

Sometimes the bridle was used in conjunction with another punishment which again mostly befell women. The ducking stool was grossly unpleasant and frequently fatal. The victim was strapped to a seat which dangled on the end of a free-moving arm and was plunged into the local pond or river. It was up to the operators of the stool as to how long she remained under the water. The shock of the cold water often killed the elderly women who found themselves in the stool. The ducking stool was used in Britain in the punishment of scolds, prostitutes and minor offenders while in America it was adopted for witches.

**THE SHOCK OF THE COLD WATER WAS OFTEN ENOUGH TO KILL THE ELDERLY WOMEN WHO FOUND THEMSELVES IN THE STOOL.**

# SKIMMINGTON RIDE

Women and men accused of infidelity or bawdy behaviour were together exposed to the ridicule of the Skimmington Ride. The punishment, imposed by outraged neighbours, had the accused pair perched back-to-back on a horse or donkey and paraded through the streets. The crowds jeered and jostled them. In Dorset the custom of 'Skimmity' included the donning of a bull's head by one of the villagers in order to taunt the accused couple. This 'beast' was known as an Ooser. In kinder times the practice of Skimmington Riding continued but the erring pair were replaced by models or masked actors.

# BURNING

To die on a pyre of dust-dry straw was an agony reserved for arsonists, heretics and witches. It was a punishment that shamed both Europe and Britain in the Middle Ages as witches and religious rebels were purged.

As witch-hunters did their dubious work, at least 200,000 died at the stake in Europe between the 11th and 18th centuries. In Britain there were sporadic witch burnings until the

handed over to the civil authorities who would burn them before the people.

Burning was therefore effectively legalised and became more frequently used in Britain. While England's kings and queens barred the Pope's Inquisitors they carried out similar barbarous punishments for similar 'crimes'.

The first victim of the 1401 Statute was William Sautre, a parish priest at Lynn, who

## AMONG THE VICTIMS WAS WARRIOR JOAN OF ARC WHO WAS BURNED BY THE BRITISH IN 1431 AS A HERETIC AND WAS CANONIZED IN 1920.

Statute of Heresy in 1401. This law enabled bishops to arrest all those believed to have spoken out against God, including preachers, schoolmasters and writers.

The onus was now on the suspect to convince the bishops that they were, in fact, devout and God-fearing. If the bishops could not be swayed then the confirmed heretic was

died in 1402. Nine years later the Prince of Wales, soon to be hero-king Henry V, watched as layman John Badby was burned alive.

The religious confusion of Henry VIII's reign had both Protestants and Catholics dying at the stake. When his daughter Mary I took the throne in 1553 the heat of religious persecution became intolerable.

# BLOODY MARY'S VICTIMS

Mary was a dour woman, devoted to the Catholic church. Her intention was to obliterate the legacy of her father in Britain, namely the Protestant Church. To this end she dispatched nearly 300 people to the stake during her five-year reign. The number included clergymen, rich men, poor men, women and even a handful of children. These dread acts earned her the title 'Bloody Mary'.

In 1849 excavations at London's Smithfield, next to St Bartholomew's Hospital, uncovered charred oak posts, a staple and a ring, surrounded by ashes and human remains. Here the 43 Smithfield Martyrs were burned at Mary's insistence.

Later in Britain, women were burned instead of being hanged, drawn and quartered, the change being introduced on the grounds of common decency. That meant women found guilty of treason or petty-treason (like the murder of a husband) would find themselves engulfed in flames.

It became customary for the victim to be strangled before being burned. This was occasionally carried out when the flames were lit. The executioner, standing some way off, pulled on a ligature tied around her neck. Sometimes a stash of gunpowder about the doomed person helped to speed their death.

Death by burning was finally abolished in Britain in 1790, with the last known case occurring in 1789.

**Above: The licking flames claim yet another martyr as religious zealotry soared in Britain during the 16th century.**

**Above right: The reign of Mary I (1553-1558) is best remembered for the spate of burnings at the stake she endorsed in order to re-instate the Catholic faith.**

# A NARROW ESCAPE

In May 1777 a girl of 14 narrowly missed a terrible death after being found guilty of debasing the coinage. She was already tied to the stake with the straw bales in place when Lord Weymouth passed by. He was horrified to see the grim penalty being carried out against one so young and intervened on her behalf.

# BURNING WITH DIGNITY

The infamous Judge Jeffreys, who dealt so ruthlessly with the prisoners taken in Monmouth's rebellion of 1685, sentenced Elizabeth Gaunt to burn on a trumped-up charge of treason. She was dragged to the stake at Tyburn on a horse-drawn hurdle before she was burned alive. A witness noted 'she met a horrible death with calmness and dignity, arranging the straw about her feet that the flames might do their work more quickly.'

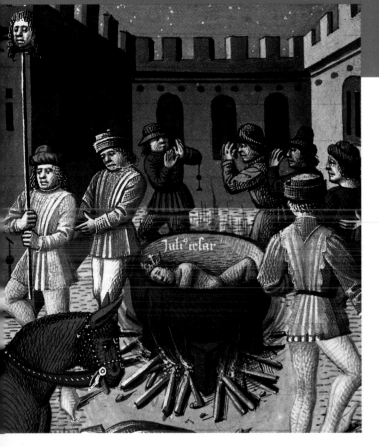

## BOILING ALIVE

King Henry VIII became famous for his sadistic cruelty. To his queens, cousins Anne Boleyn and Catherine Howard, he was merciless. And he was savage with his people, too, as an Act passed in 1531 reveals. This permitted those convicted of poisoning to be boiled alive.

A maid was killed in a cauldron of boiling water in the same year the Act was introduced. Richard Roose, a cook who poisoned the soup at the Bishop of Rochester's palace, shared the same miserable fate on 15 April 1532. Two people died because of Roose although the Bishop himself survived. Roose was taken to Smithfield where he was boiled alive. A further case is recorded in March 1542 when maid Margaret Davy died, also at Smithfield.

To the relief of all, the statute which legalised boiling alive was abolished when King Henry died and his son Edward VI came to the throne.

**Left: A cauldron became a coffin for those sentenced to boiling alive.**

**Right: Last rites before the garrotte squeezes the life from its victims.**

## THE WHEEL

In France and Germany the wheel was a popular form of capital punishment, not least because it was pure agony for the victim. In concept it was similar to a crucifixion. The prisoner was brought to the scaffold where his cloak was ripped off, to reveal nothing but a pair of brief linen pants.

The prisoner was then tied to the side of the wheel lying on the scaffold, stretched across its spokes and hub. Now the executioner advanced wielding an iron bar. His brief was to shatter the limbs one by one with the hefty weapon. Each arm and leg was broken in several places before the job was done. A skilled executioner would smash the bones of his victim without piercing the skin. The wheel was then propped upright so onlookers could appreciate the dying gasps of the victim.

At first the severity of the injuries was thought to be sufficient to bring about death. Later the executioner ended the torture by one or two blows to the chest. The wheel could be refined, too, to include other torturous aspects. A suspended wheel might be turned over a fire or a bed of nails. In any event it meant unbearable suffering for the victim.

## STRANGULATION

Centuries ago the garrotte was merely hanging by another name. But, during the Middle Ages, executioners began to refine the use of the rope until it became as feared and as vile as any punishment of that dark era. European executioners first used the garotte to end the suffering of men broken on the wheel, but by the turn of the 18th century the seed of an idea involving slow strangulation was planted in the minds of Euope's law-makers.

### THE EXECUTIONER MERELY PULLED VERY HARD ON BOTH ENDS OF THE CORDS, SLOWLY CHOKING THE PRISONER.

The first models were ruthlessly simple. They consisted of an upright post with a hole bored through it. The victim stood or sat on a wooden seat in front of the post and a cord was looped around his or her neck, with its free ends feeding through the hole. The executioner merely pulled very hard on both ends of the cords, slowly choking the prisoner.

A modified design used a stick to twist and tighten the ropes. Later designs replaced the rope with an iron collar. A screw was driven into the collar to throttle the victim.

More sophisticated still was the garrotte with two metal neck rings. The screw propelled one collar back towards the post and

# UTION

the other forwards, parting the vertebrae and causing instant death. Another variation employed a small, sharp blade to sever the spinal cord.

The garrotte was adopted as the means of capital punishment in Spain. Treatment on the garrotte was preceded by a mind-numbing ritual in which the prisoner was taken from his cell – and told to bid it farewell for ever – before being led in a night of intense prayer by two or more clergymen. He was implored to repent to secure a place in heaven. In the morning he was asked to confess his crime. Spanish law did not allow the execution to go ahead until a confession was illicited. Usually, the admission was forthcoming.

## THE MAZZATELLO

In Italy the most crude death penalty of all flourished. Even a truly bloodthirsty audience must have been repelled at seeing the infamous Mazzatello in action.

To inflict this punishment the executioner needed nothing more than a huge mallet, sometimes known as the mazza, and a knife. The prisoner was led by a clergyman to the scaffold set up in a prominent place. Facing the doomed man was the masked executioner dressed in black and the coffin he would soon be occupying. The victim was positioned facing the crowd.

Then the executioner would pounce from behind, clouting the prisoner as hard as he could with the mazza. With his prey unconscious on the floor and probably suffering from a shattered skull, the executioner would produce a knife and slit the prisoner's throat. It was a popular death penalty in the Papal States and it was not until the patriot Garibaldi united Italy that the custom was dropped once and for all.

# SSING CASES

## ERS WHO REFUSED TO PLEAD WERE
## D TO THE FLOOR UNDER IRON WEIGHTS.
## ICE WAS SIMPLE – SUBMIT OR DIE.

Old English courts were in a quandary if suspects refused to plead to the charges that were laid against them.

It was simple enough if prisoners admitted their crimes. The law stepped in, confiscated their estates and meted out punishment – more often than not the death penalty. If the crime was denied, a trial would ensue. Once again, if

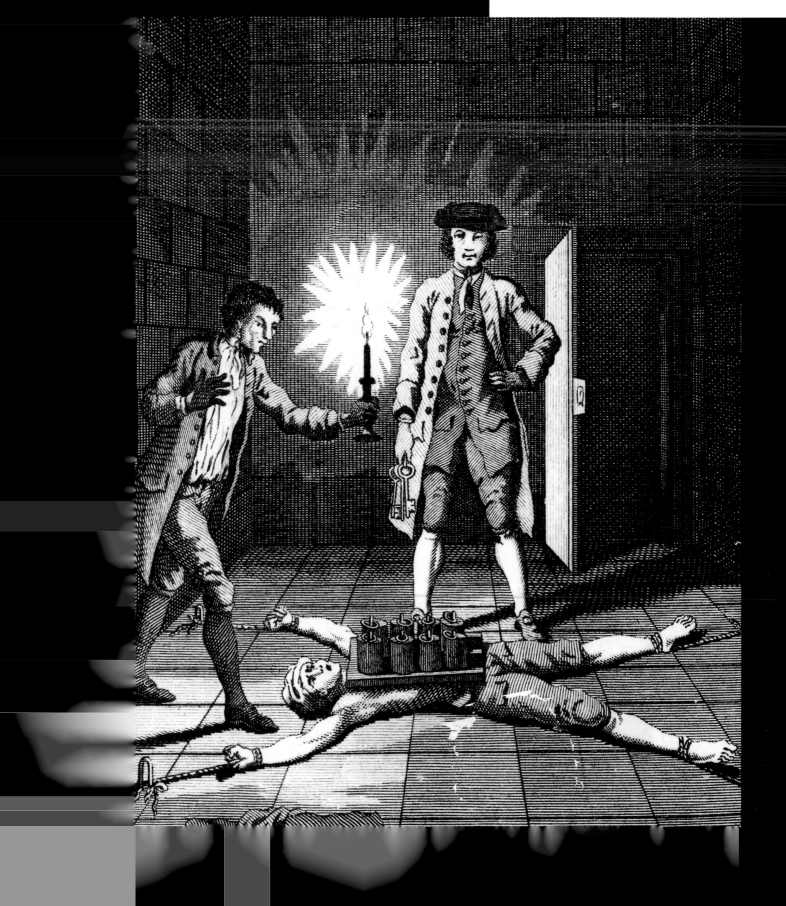

found guilty, the convict would be punished and forfeit all possessions to the Crown.

Yet defendants might decide to remain mute. That way they would stay unconvicted – as it was not until 1827 that silence by a defendant was construed in law as a 'not guilty' plea. Before that time, their property and goods could not be touched. So their families enjoyed a degree of protection and could continue life much as before.

It was a powerful incentive for many not to plead after arrest. The law decided on an equally persuasive method of forcing a plea. That method was *peine forte et dure* (the strong and hard pain), quite literally pressing to death. The victim would be spread-eagled on the floor of a cell, then weights piled up on him or her. It was an agonising choice for the victim – to plead or die. This sentence was handed down with chilling words:

'That you be taken back to the prison whence you came, to a low dungeon into which no light can enter; that you be laid upon your back on the bare floor with a cloth round your loins but elsewhere naked; that there be set upon your body a weight or iron as great as you can bear, and greater. That you have no sustenance save on the first day three morsels of the coarsest barley (bread); on the second day three draughts of stagnant water; on the third day bread as before; next day water as before; until you die.'

The intention was to illicit a guilty plea from the prisoner, at which point the pressing was halted, the weights removed and the gasping fellow returned to the court.

# PHYSICAL ENDURANCE

Edward III granted a pardon to suspected killer Cecilia Rygeway, who was thought to have murdered her husband John, after she survived a pressing in Nottingham jail which lasted 40 days. She was even deprived of the morsels of bread and puddle water customarily given. The words of the pardon describe her survival 'after the manner of a miracle and contrary to human nature'.

# HANGING IN TATTERS

Nathaniel Hawes refused to plead at his trial in 1721 because his fine suit of clothes had been stolen. 'I will not plead for no one shall say that I was hanged in a dirty shirt and ragged coat,' he declared. When 250 lb (113 kg) was piled on his chest he had a change of heart. He was found guilty and was hanged in tatters.

# PRESSED TO DEATH

On 23 April 1605 Walter Calverley, in a fit of jealous and drink-induced madness, killed his two sons and his wife at the family home, Calverley Hall, in Yorkshire. His intention was to kill a surviving son, Henry, but he was arrested before he could do so. Incarcerated at York Castle, the elder Calverley refused to plead, entirely so his son Henry could inherit his goods and estate. In August he was pressed to death, an unconvicted man.

In 1672 at the Monmouth Assizes, Henry Jones refused to plead and was sentenced to be pressed. His agony began on a Saturday, the day after he appeared in court, and he did not die until midday on Monday.

*Peine forte et dure* was adopted as a judicial measure during the 14th century and enjoyed its heyday in the reign of Henry IV at the beginning of the 15th century. It was not until 1772 that this barbaric practice was abolished by law in Britain.

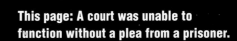

This page: A court was unable to function without a plea from a prisoner.

Opposite page: Inside the press room at Newgate Prison, deprived of daylight and fresh air, a prisoner is put under pressure. Outside, the court authorities awaited a change of heart.

# MARGARET
## THE MARTYR

**FOR DEVOUT CATHOLICS THESE WERE DARK DAYS. NO ONE WAS SAFE FROM THOSE WHO POLICED THE NATION'S RELIGIOUS LEANINGS – AT THIS TIME RABIDLY PROTESTANT. EVEN THE MOST PIOUS AND GOOD RISKED A TERRIBLE FATE.**

**Torturers used every means at their disposal to change the hue of their victim's faith. Still, many refused to deny the religion they held dear and suffered the consequences.**

Yorkshire-born Margaret Clitherow endured pain and suffocation under a pile of rocks by order of the courts. Her crime was commitment to the Catholic faith in Elizabethan times when the fervour for Protestantism was rife.

On 1 July 1571 Margaret, then aged 18, married John Clitherow at St Martin's Church. Her groom was a well-known local butcher who took her to live in The Shambles, one of York's most famous old streets. She frequently helped out in the shop, although the family were not short of money.

She had heard a diatribe against the Catholic faith for years from her converted stepfather, Henry May, an ambitious innkeeper. But she began to doubt the words of disparagement against the Pope and his followers. The conflict in her mind in 1572 was sharpened by the execution of Thomas Percy, the seventh Earl of Northumberland, only yards from her home.

Even if she didn't attend the axing, she most certainly would have heard the bays and roars of the crowd as the executioner hoisted the severed head above his own. Percy had led forces loyal to the Catholic faith against Protestant Queen Elizabeth. Even as his head lay on the block, he refused to acknowledge the Protestant Church.

Margaret took her first steps towards Catholicism at a time when links with Rome were considered treason. The penalty for a woman who remained true to her Catholic faith was usually death by burning. She joined a covert network of Catholics around the city, holding Masses and sheltering priests. So devoted was she to the Church that she even sent away her eldest son John to receive a Catholic education in France.

## A HARSH SENTENCE

Frustrated, Judge John Clench finally decreed she would be pressed to death. Margaret's response was to thank God. The city was shocked at the Draconian penalty issued against Margaret Clitherow, step-daughter of the Lord Mayor and wife of an eminent citizen. Friends soon began a rumour that she was pregnant, hopeful that this would delay the execution, but the ploy failed.

The council sent a volley of men to her to illicit a denial of Rome. None succeeded. Even the pain of leaving husband and children was not enough to compel her to fly in the face of her religion.

On 25 March 1586 Margaret, wearing a flimsy gown, was taken to die at the Tollbooth, six yards outside the prison. She and the womenfolk accompanying her begged

**Pope Paul VI recognised the suffering endured by Margaret Clitherow and made her a saint.**

that she should die in the white gown she had bought into prison for the purpose. The request was turned down. She laid down on the ground, covered her face with a handkerchief, her privacy only protected by the gown laid across her. Both hands were tied to posts to make her body the shape of a cross. A stone the size of a fist was put under her back.

She once again refused to change her views and the first weight was laid on her. By nine o'clock that morning, about eight hundred-weight (0.4 tonnes) was in place. The stones crushed her ribs which pierced the skin. Within 15 minutes she was dead.

Margaret the martyr was beatified in 1929 and made a saint by Pope Paul VI in 1970. She is one of 40 martyrs who is remembered on October 25.

That triggered betrayal by her stepfather, the boy's godfather and soon-to-be Lord Mayor of the city. Embarrassed by her antics, he was convinced Margaret could be cowed into accepting the Protestant religion. However, he reckoned without her stalwart character. Margaret was arrested after a search party burst into her home and found evidence of her harbouring priests. She appeared before the York Lent Assizes in 1586. Against the pin-sharp legal minds of the day, she constantly denied the charges against her – and refused to deny her religion and convert to her stepfather's faith.

# FRENCH BLOOD LUST

**IN PRE-REVOLUTIONARY FRANCE EXECUTIONS WERE, OF COURSE, PUBLIC AND THEY WERE ALSO VERY SLOW. SOMETIMES IT TOOK MORE THAN 24 HOURS FOR THE VICTIM TO DIE.**

In some countries, sensitivities were offended by the use of torture and it was not permitted in the pursuit of justice. In France where conviction hinged on confession it was a different story. To win the necessary admission the authorities readily resorted to torture. It was a grim fate that awaited suspected criminals in pre-revolutionary France. Executions were, of course, public and they were also very slow. Sometimes it took more than 24 hours for the victim to die.

The ritual of the execution began when the criminal was taken from his home past the scene of his crime to the nearest venue for torture. For maximum effect the authorities swooped at night and dragged the villain through the town in a daunting torch-lit procession. He was tortured until he confessed.

Once the confession had been made the convict was isolated during what was called 'the sleepless night'. The theory was that he should spend the night considering the enormity of his crime and seeking God's forgiveness. In practice it was the time when he would be expected to implicate accomplices.

Thereafter he would be taken to court and from there to his execution. The procession to the scaffold was deemed an important feature of the punishment. It heaped humiliation on the shoulders of the doomed man and served as a warning to others. Wearing a shirt and a rope around his neck, the prisoner carried a board declaring his felony. When it was time to mount the scaffold he had the opportunity to denounce once again his accomplices or make a final request.

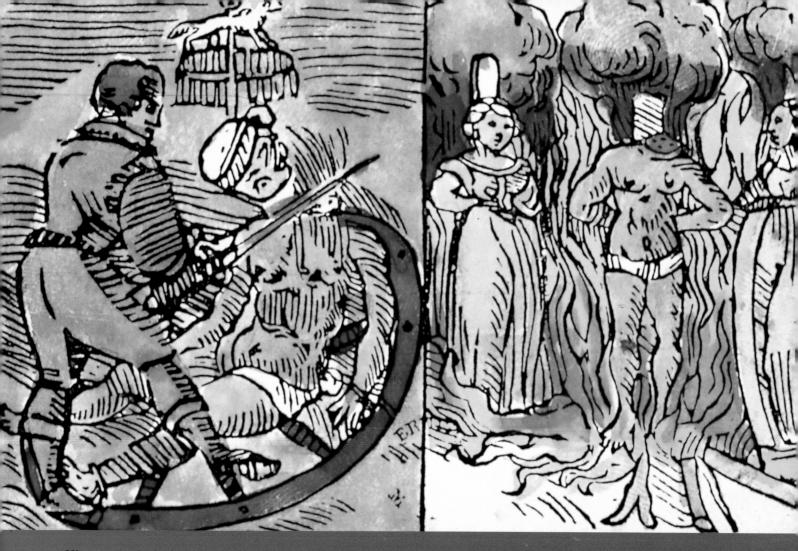

Miscreants who had previously been before a judge for sentencing were slowly broken on the wheel. When the release of death occurred the accused was killed by a blow to the chest or, as here, decapitated. Afterwards, his body was often burnt at the stake.

## THEATRE OF DEATH

Only the lucky were hanged. Punishment in France was ostentatious and spectacular. The aim was to make an impact on the throng which gathered to watch. At the crux of French justice was a conflict of power, with on one side the sovereign and on the other the criminal. French philosopher Michel Foucault, who died in 1984, described it as a war waged between the king and the convict. To illustrate the king's triumph, the criminal was marked. Branding was often followed by death on the wheel.

Gradually, the masses came to reject excessive and violent punishment. Some convicts were heroes. Their antics had pleased rather than appalled the people and nobody wanted to see them hang. There were increasing numbers of scaffold riots. Sometimes the wooden steps of the gallows were sawn off and occasionally the convict was kidnapped.

In 1757 Robert Damiens tried to kill Louis XV. The French judicial system went into punishment overdrive. First Damiens was mutilated with red hot tongs then scalded with burning oil. Finally he was ripped apart by four strong horses. While the people were sympathetic toward the king he misunderstood their response. This callous punishment had gone beyond acceptable levels. Although the death of Damiens did not induce revolutionary fervour it did illustrate how the people now sought a balance between acceptance of the monarch's power and the boundary of his excesses.

## FRENCH FOLK HERO

France's favourite folk hero was the robber Cartouche. During the 1720s poverty was widespread and previously honest men were compelled to take up crime in order to feed their families. Against this background the resourceful Cartouche found many accomplices. It took the police three years to find Cartouche and he was ultimately executed in Paris. But his popularity lived on. In this war between king and convict, the convict was held victor.

# INQUISITION

By dictionary definition, a heretic is a 'holder of an unorthodox opinion'. It is not, by any rational measure, a crime which merits torture or punishment of death.

Yet an outbreak of paranoia in the Roman Catholic church of the 13th century sparked a passionate war against heretics which brought thousands of lives to a grisly end. Like so many zealous dogmas, it began with a spark of virtue but ended as an orgy of killing.

# THE WRATH OF ROME

**THE CHURCH WAS RICH AND GREEDY AND MANY OF ITS MONKS WERE LASCIVIOUS, THIEVING, CORRUPT AND EVEN VIOLENT.**

Trouble brewed for the Roman Catholic Church in the 11th century with the growing popularity of heretic creeds. It is hardly surprising that people turned against Rome. The church was rich and greedy and many of its monks were lascivious, thieving, corrupt and even violent. Traditional Christian values of meekness, poverty and humility were scarcely found among Catholic clerics.

It was only a matter of time before the flock began to question the wisdom of the masters of Rome who had thus far enjoyed domination of the Christian world. Their power, their very future, was in peril.

# THE ALBIGENSES

A heretical sect called the Cathari spread through Europe from Bulgaria in the 11th century. In the French town of Albi people were ready to accept its doctrine and a new sect flourished as a result.

The Albigenses believed that, while the material world was on the whole evil, the human soul was good and would be reunited with God. Virginity and poverty were lauded qualities, while riches and warfare were abhorred. Like the Cathari – taken from the Greek word for 'the pure' – the Albigenses heartily disliked the pomp and ritual of the Roman Catholic Church and questioned its right to religious rule.

When the popular preacher St Bernard of Clairvaux visited southern France in 1147 he found Catholic Churches empty. In the eyes of Rome, the new religion threatened to spread over Europe as rampantly and disastrously as a plague. The consternation of the Catholic church was even greater because Albi, in the Languedoc region, was wealthy. The Papal coffers would be badly hit if its residents turned their backs on the church of Rome.

In 1207 Pierre de Castlenau, Chief Legate to Pope Innocent III, was murdered. The prime suspect was publicly announced by Rome to be Raymond, Count of Toulouse, who ruled in the Albigenses heartland. This was tantamount to an invitation to the princes and knights loyal to Rome to attack Albi. Given its riches, they needed no further encouragement.

**A stonework relief of the siege of Toulouse depicts the violence and cruelty employed by Rome to silence the heretics.**

## CRUSADES OF BUTCHERS

A crusade led by the elder Simon de Montfort did much to destroy the sect. An estimated 20,000 knights and 200,000 foot soldiers attempted to scourge the area of Albigenses, wreaking havoc as they went. The falsely accused Raymond gave himself up to the soldiers of Rome in order to spare his people. He was tortured and executed without trial, shabby treatment which roused the wrath of the King of France. The crusade was duly halted. But greedy knights and fanatical monks were not satisfied and told their Holy Father so. A further crusade was summoned by the Pope in 1214 and the butchery continued. Heretic knights were hanged by the score. Women and children were once again stoned to death and cast down deep wells in the pitiless rampage.

When soldiers asked one of the Crusade leaders, the disreputable Abbot of Citeaux, how they might distinguish between Catholics and heretics, he told them: 'Kill them all, God will know his own.' Without doubt, decent Catholic folk were slaughtered by their kinsmen. Of course, persecution only served to inspire and consolidate the faith of the heretics. Those that escaped would become fodder for the soon-to-be created Inquisition.

# THE WALDENSIANS

As the 13th century got under way rich merchant Peter Waldo of Lyons (right) re-examined his lifestyle and found it wanting. Accordingly, Waldo, who died in 1217, gave away his worldly goods to live a life of poverty in the French Alps. The community he formed was known as the 'poor men of Lyons', the Vaudois or the Waldensians.

The Waldensians were in opposition to Rome because they adhered to the teaching of the Bible, not the Pope. They did not believe in celibacy for clergymen or purgatory. Like the Albigenses, the Waldensians were persecuted by the Inquisition and the group scattered over Europe and later reached America. There are about 20,000 Waldensians today.

# THE CHURCH TAKES OVER THE

## INQUISITION

**THE INQUISITION OR 'HOLY OFFICE' GAINED MOMENTUM DURING THE EARLY YEARS OF THE 13TH CENTURY. WITHIN A FEW DECADES IT LEFT SCARS ALL OVER EUROPE.**

For the crusades against the Albigenses the Pope relied on secular forces to carry out his will. However, he knew they might never again be so obliging. Certainly, there were sporadic outbursts of violence against heretics in the 10th and 11th centuries unprompted by Rome – but they barely tackled the mushrooming popularity of the heretics. Pope Innocent III realised his church was exposed and vulnerable and decided it was time to instigate a church-run campaign to eradicate heresy once and for all.

With four decrees issued between 1204 and 1213 he empowered bishops to seek out heresy in named venues, rather than wait for it to manifest itself. Special holy officials, known as 'Inquisitors' were employed for the purposes of the investigations.

Yet it is Innocent's successor who is generally credited with firing the first salvoes of the fully-fledged Inquisition. Pope Gregory IX established the Inquisition by 1230. He had already indicated his tough stance when he formally endorsed the death penalty for heretics adopted in Lombardy in 1224, clearly setting the tone for the rest of Europe.

Bishops had proved unwilling and unreliable in the thrust against heretics. So Dominican and Franciscan friars were given the task. They tackled it with gusto and relish.

At first the task of torturing fell to laymen. But a Papal Bull of 1256 allowed the churchmen, in the interests of efficiency, to carry out the job themselves.

Through the Inquisition the Catholic Church had an excellent formula to meet its own ends. Now it had the seek-and-find powers which could not be entrusted to the secular authorities. It was up to the Inquisitors to exact a confession and the way they got it was their business. Inquisitors were not concerned with the civil and moral rights of suspects.

Along the way, the wealth of the church would be enhanced with the riches and land confiscated from heretics. (The local bishops also received a cut, which helped to keep them sweet, as did the Inquisitors themselves.) However, the church handed the confessed heretic over to the civil authorities for ultimate punishment so its clerics kept blood from their hands, in public at least.

Inquisitors moved town-by-town across Europe, bearing a golden crucifix above their heads. When they arrived they would meet with the bishop, his clergy and local people. Their brief was to weed out heretics and locals were told that names of known offenders should be shared in confidence with them. There was a month's grace given for heretics to give themselves up.

These were the lucky ones. Those who immediately confessed were brought back into the fold after renouncing their former beliefs. As a penalty they might have to pray, fast, pay a fine or take a pilgrimage.

**Pope Gregory IX, who died in 1241 aged 99 years, is credited with launching the Inquisition. He believed anyone who veered from the Catholic faith should die.**

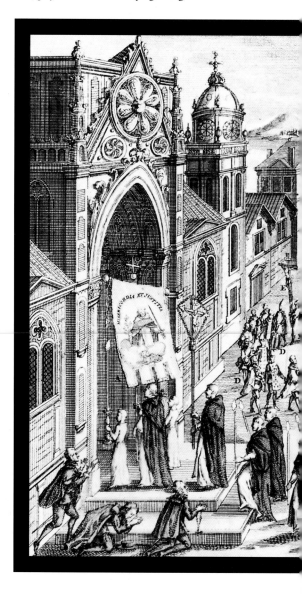

## SECRET DENUNCIATIONS

For the rest a grinding and relentless horror began. Fertile minds among the population were happy to denounce members of their community. Never mind that a feud between accused and accuser had been running for generations. The friars listened to one and all, even convicted criminals whose evidence would have been immediately disregarded as unreliable in other judicial systems. The accused was never told who had denounced him or her and accordingly could not mount a defence.

It only needed two like-minded witnesses for the Inquisitors to be convinced of guilt. These were easy enough to find. One accuser would name a fellow witness. If that person failed to concur he was tortured until he did. Alternatively, bribery might secure a second denunciation. Legal assistance for the accused was barred by the Pope himself, for anyone who defended a heretic was guilty himself of that crime.

The first tentative step was to confine the accused to his home. Two visitors then put him through 'the third degree', a bitter interrogation. If he still denied heresy he was summoned to the Inquisition.

**Below, left: In villages, towns and cities the arrival of the Inquisition was marked with a parade.**

**Below: Friars set themselves up as judges and juries. They sought confession . . . by any means.**

## COURTS OF THE INQUISITION

When the Inquisition arrived in a town it appointed a jury to man its independent courts. Between 20 and 50 'good and experienced' men were to assist the monks in reaching their verdicts. Most were priests while there was room for the occasional sympathetic layman like lawyers. All they had to prove was that they were rabidly anti-heretic and thus in total accord with the Inquisitors. Guilt was proved by the existence of the two witnesses, not decided by the jury. The jury never conflicted with the friars.

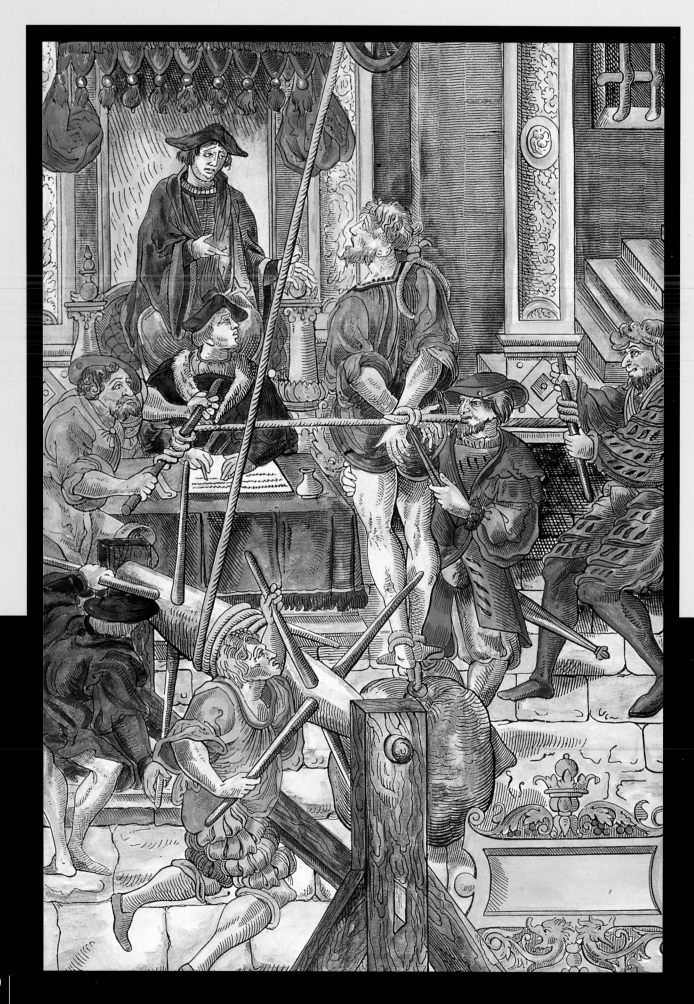

# THE INQUISITORS' WORK

## HIDEOUSLY UNJUST AND PSYCHOTIC IN THEIR DEVOTION TO DUTY, THE INQUISITORS WENT TO ANY LENGTHS TO WRING CONFESSIONS FROM THEIR VICTIMS.

Hideously unjust and psychotic in their devotion to duty, the Inquisitors went to any lengths to wring confessions from their victims.

Anyone who denied being a heretic was tortured. Among the devices the monks had at hand were the rack which would pull the limbs in different directions until tendons tore or bones cracked. There was the strappado in which the accused was suspended by his wrists and heavy weights attached to his ankles. In its most extreme form, the ropes of the strappado were jerked violently downwards, dislocating the bound arms of the victim. This was called squassation. Prisoners were clapped in an 'iron boot' and then had wedges of wood had hammered between their skin and the metal. The array of implements available to Inquisitors also included the lash, thumbscrews, hot pincers and a brazier of burning coals. In addition there was water torture, in which the victim might be forced to swallow or breathe in water until he felt he was drowning.

If the confession of heresy was not forthcoming, then the accused clearly would not renounce his alternative faith. Those heretics who did not confess were paraded through the streets in marked garments before being handed over to the secular authorities to be burned at the stake. While the number burned at the stake might have been relatively few, many died during torture or in the hellish Papal prisons. To survive it was essential to confess to heresy before being judged as a heretic.

Of course, many victims broke and confessed to heresy. Yet confession might not mark the end of their plight. The Inquisitors wanted the names of their cohorts and would continue torturing until they got them.

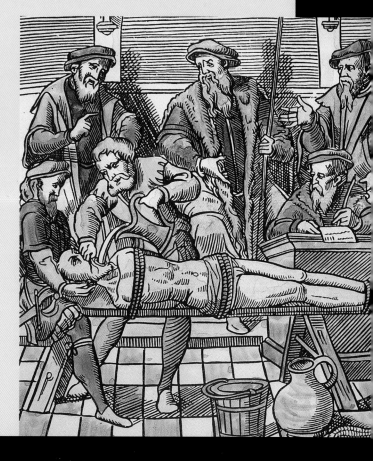

**Above, right: Victims subjected to water torture were plied with liquid until they felt they were drowning.**

**Opposite page: A wooden relief made in 1541 illustrates the 'estrapade', in which the victim was bound and hoisted before the clerics of the Inquisition.**

## BERNARD GUI

Inquisitor Bernard Gui, of France, declared 88 dead men were heretics during his career and sought revenge on their dry bones. A further 548 people were burned alive at the stake at his behest.

## EVEN THE DEAD WERE UNSAFE

Such was the frenzy inspired by the Inquisition that dead men were named as heretics. This was a disaster for their living relatives. Not only was the corpse dug up, paraded through the town and burned at the stake but the estate and wealth of his descendants was seized. Here was punishment brought against those who could not defend themselves, illustrating the Inquisition's disregard for justice.

Those that confessed after torture were fined by the Inquisitors. Anyone who could not afford to pay was thrown in jail. The Inquisitors' prisons were notorious. Still suffering the effects of the torture, the victim would be dumped in a stinking dungeon. Sometimes the penalty included solitary confinement. If not he would be hung up in chains next to others, left to beg for bread and water. Although saved the horror of the stake, death was protracted and agonising.

On a Sunday morning the doomed heretics were handed over to the authorities for their ultimate punishment. Without a trace of irony, the Inquisitors appealed for clemency. None was given for there was an unspoken rule that the magistrates or royal houses in charge of proceedings would be excommunicated from the Catholic Church without ado if the death sentence was not hastily carried out.

Too late, Rome realised that a monster had been created. Pope Clement V tried to curb the bloodlust by declaring that the accused should be tortured once only. The Inquisitors' response was to continue that torture session day-in, day-out

**Left:** Until the 14th century the Templars were widely regarded as heroes. Their success during the crusades had given them wealth which had grown over the years . . . such wealth surely led to envy.

**Right:** Jaques de Molay, the last master of the Knights Templars, was burnt at the stake and the King of France won his battle to obliterate the order.

# KNIGHTS
## TEMPLARS

After the Christian Crusades had triumphed over the Muslims in Jerusalem, a new holy order for knights was born. The year was 1118 and times were still treacherous. Devout knight Huges de Payen gathered about 40 like-minded veterans around him to form the order of the Knights Templars.

So noble were the knights that they each took monastic vows of personal poverty. They refused to associate with women and placed great value on the qualities of courage and valour. For their seal the Templars chose a picture of two knights on a horse – to indicate that they had renounced earthly riches.

The Order's first task was to make the bandit-lined roads to Jerusalem safe for pilgrims to travel along. Thanks to this heroism, King Baldwin II of Jerusalem gave them a wing of his palace, the Temple of Solomon. Thereafter their full name was The Order of the Poor Knights of the Temple of Solomon.

However, it was a struggle to survive in the far-flung reaches of Christendom so in 1126 Huge de Payen travelled to Europe where the order began to prosper. From 1128 the knights wore a white tunic, offered to them by Pope Honorius. The red cross emblazoned on it, which became a familiar hallmark, was added in 1146. The reputation of the knights spread throughout Europe during the 12th century, as did the influence of their powerful patron St Bernard of Clairvaux.

## 'THE INQUISITION WAS INVENTED TO ROB THE RICH OF THEIR POSSESSIONS.'
## SEGNI, 16TH CENTURY WRITER

## KNIGHTS V INQUISITION

Crusades came and went and the Knights Templars, now spread over Europe, took an active part. They were ever ready to make war with the 'infidels' in the east. Yet as time went by the Order lost sight of its original purpose. A new role emerged, that of international banker. Whether by accident or design, the Order accrued great wealth and privilege which did not go unnoticed. As the 14th century dawned King Philip the Fair of France cast greedy eyes on the riches of the Knights Templars and decided that their wealth should be his. The Inquisition was a convenient cudgel with which to beat the Knights Templars and get what he wanted.

Never before was the paradox of the Inquisition so clearly illustrated. Here were a band of men who had always been loyal to the Pope. True, the initial function of the Knights was gone. But countless

Then King Philip branded them heretics. His accusation was that the Templars worshipped a devilish idol called Baphomet which had the appearance of a goat-headed man. They spat on the cross, he claimed, and carried out homosexual acts.

There was no truth in the allegations but it made no difference. King Philip made his first move against them on 12 October 1307 when he seized their properties. There then followed the familiar process of accusation,

## DEATH OF THE TEMPLARS

No fewer than 36 Knights Templars died under torture in Paris. Scores more were burned at the stake. As knight refused to condemn brother knight the suffering was immense. On 2 May 1313 Pope Clement published a Papal Bull against the Order which was to signify its demise. Its last master, Jacques de Molay, was burned at the stake and with him

# PUNISHMENT OF GENIUS

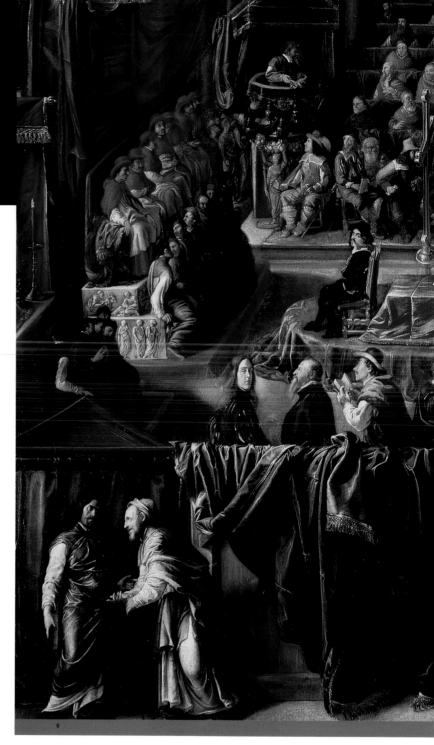

Shamefully the Inquisition was used to shackle the progress of science and shadow the world from enlightenment. Such was Rome's lust for power that it refused to recognise landmark discoveries unless they were proven in the Bible and endorsed by the Pope.

The infallibility of the Pope was central to the Catholic faith. The finders of new facts or figures which contradicted those existing were branded as heretics. That's how Medieval genius Galileo Galilei found himself on the wrong side of the church.

Galileo was already an accomplished scientist when he built himself a telescope in

## 'EPPUR SI MUOVE',
### MEANING 'STILL THE EARTH MOVES'. GALILEO'S REACTION TO THE CHURCH'S RULING ON HIS THEORY.

1609. His studies of the stars proved beyond doubt that the earth was orbiting the sun. It was a point of view already put forward by Nicolaus Copernicus, a Polish astronomer who hit on the 'earth-in-motion' revelations while drawing up planetary charts. The only problem was that the church believed the earth was stationary at the centre of the universe and that the sun moved around it.

Wisely, Copernicus had kept his own counsel, sharing his views with only a few close friends. The full text of his book *De revolutionibus orbium coelstium* was not published until 1543, the year he died. Legend says he received the first copy on his death bed.

Galileo was mindful that, in the words of one eminent Cardinal: 'The Bible is intended to teach us how to go to heaven, not how the heavens go.' But torn between faith and fact, he found himself unable to appease the church by denying the discovery. He continually brought the debate to the top of the agenda. In 1614 he wrote his famous *Letter to Castelli* which propounded his theories.

**Galileo, one of the greatest minds of the 17th century, was cowed in a courtroom into accepting Papal Bull.**

## INQUISITION FORCED TO ACT

Outraged clerics sent a copy to the Roman Inquisition. There was little in its content to concern the church so the matter against Galileo was dropped. One officious Dominican priest, Thomas Caccini, persisted and visited Rome to testify personally against Galileo. Again, no action was taken – but alarm bells were now sounding in the Vatican.

Galileo had his champions, among them the future Pope Urban VIII, but the number of his detractors in the Church grew. When the frustrated scientist beat a path to Rome to put his case, Pope Paul V referred the matter to the Inquisition. Galileo was on trial, perhaps for his life. Theological experts from the ranks

## POSTHUMOUS PARDON

After the second trial the Inquisition found Galileo was 'vehemently suspected of heresy'. In a bid to heal the divide between church and science, Pope John Paul II instituted an investigation. Galileo was finally cleared of heresy by a Vatican commission in 1992.

of the Inquisition decided the Copernican theory was 'foolish and absurd, philosophically and formally heretical inasmuch as it expressly contradicts the doctrine of Holy Scripture in many passages . . .'

In judgement, the cardinals stopped short of accusing Galileo of heresy. However, he was told 'to abstain altogether from teaching or defending (Copercanism) and even from discussing it.' Galileo was furious. He insisted on having a certificate from Rome which forbade him to 'hold or defend' the controversial doctrine – although the Vatican refused to acknowledge the irony of it.

For 16 years Galileo was gagged. But in 1632 he published the witty *Dialogue on the Two Great World Systems* which poked fun at the antiquated Church view. Galileo thought the acid humour would side-step the ban. He was wrong.

For the second time Galileo was summoned to the Inquisition. This time he was 68 years old with failing health. Hanging over him was the threat of torture and Galileo duly recanted his views. He was sentenced to spend the rest of his days under house arrest, forbidden again to talk about the movement of the planets. He died in his bed in 1642.

# INQUISITION TO
# WITCH HUNT

**Innocent VIII was horrified by an epidemic of witches in Europe.**

While once the world seemed peopled with heretics, now it was swarming with witches. During two and a half centuries of 'witch fever' the Inquisition found apparently endless suspects, nowhere more so than Germany, where 100,000 were burned at the stake.

Until the Inquisition turned its attentions to witches they were regarded as inoffensive and occasionally helpful, the suppliers of lotions and potions and the tellers of fortunes. The putrid minds of the friars had them in partnership with the Devil. And it was the influence of the monks that counted.

Numerous disasters, major and minor, were now laid at the door of witches: a failed harvest, an outbreak of disease, a lame horse or even burnt bread. In the superstitious minds of peasant folk, these occurrences were the result

## DUCKING

One 'foolproof' way to establish whether a suspect was a witch was ducking. With right thumb bound to left toe, the accused was plunged into a convenient pond. If he or she floated it proved an association with the black arts, with the body rejecting the baptismal water. If the victim drowned they were innocent. Given the curious position of the prisoner, it was more likely they would float.

There was a guide available for Inquisitors called *Malleus Maleficarum* or *Hammer of Witches* setting out the guidelines for interrogation techniques. The authors were Dominican friars Heinrich Kramer and Jakob Sprenger, both ruthless inquisitors. Kramer had been ousted from his powerbase in the Tyrol by his bishop for trickery. He had hidden a woman in an oven and when she denounced local people from her hiding place he claimed these were the words of the Devil.

## GERMAN ATROCITIES

In 22 villages near Trier in the Rhineland a total of 368 women were burned within six years – and two of the worst-hit villages were left with just a single female resident apiece.

While burning at the stake was the fate of most witches, more imaginative minds devised their own horrific variants on the death penalty. In an oven built at Neisse in Silesia during the middle of the 17th century the executioner roasted more than two thousand women and girls in nine years, including two babies.

Within eight years the Bishop of Wurzburg burned more than 900 convicted witches at the stake, including lawyers, clerics, noblemen and children as young as seven years old – nobody was safe. So blackhearted was he that he had his own nephew beheaded for alleged witchcraft. Meanwhile the corrupt bishop grew rich on the confiscated wealth and property of his victims.

In Bamberg new tortures were invented in a chamber built into the bishop's home. They included burning the prisoner's groin, scalding lime baths and force feeding on salt foods without water.

Witch-hunter Franz Buirmann, of Cologne, arrested one woman as a witch after she refused his amorous advances. She was tortured, raped by the torturer's assistant and then burned alive.

## SEARCH FOR A SIGN

Suspected witches were stripped, shaved then strapped in a chair for questioning. It was believed that all witches had a familiar – a demon in animal form. So, one way to establish that a suspect was a witch, was to gain evidence of a familiar. The suspect was left strapped to a chair in a cell while the Inquisitors watched and waited. Should a beetle, mouse or rat enter the cell (which was likely as the prisons were infested with vermin) and approach the shivering figure then this proved the accused guilty.

The naked body of the accused was minutely examined as the Inquisitors sought a witch's or Devil's mark. A witch's mark stuck out like a nipple. The Devil's mark was a spot, scar, birthmark – and could even be invisible! It was a mark of ownership left by the Devil.

A pin stuck in this mark would cause neither pain nor bleeding, the believers convinced themselves. To be sure of a conviction, many Inquisitors used knives with retractable blades when they speared the Devil's mark. That way there was no sensation in the victim and no blood.

Giant balance scales could also help identify a witch. If the suspect was heavier than the weights – sometimes a Bible was used instead of weights – then he or she was clearly a witch. Only if a perfect balance was struck was the accused vindicated. This rarely, if ever, occurred.

**Lurid paintings of wild orgies supposedly held on the Witches' Sabbath helped justify extreme measures against witches.**

of a curse issued by a disgruntled witch. If a mishap blighted a family they were keen to denounce anyone they suspected of witchcraft in the neighbourhood.

Witches were thought to copulate with the devil, to kill babies and drink their blood, to trample on the cross and to summon up demons at will. Crimes such as these were so heinous that the Inquisitors felt justified in paying informers in areas where denunciations were thin. Given the penalty for witchcraft was burning at the stake, most hauled into court on the say-so of someone else quickly denied the charges levelled against them. Then the torture began.

# THE WITCH-FINDER

Scourge of witches in 17th century England was Matthew Hopkins, the self-styled 'Witch-finder General'.

Hopkins began his disgraceful career in Manningtree, a remote town on the plains of East Anglia. It was 1644 and the Puritans were in power. Failed lawyer Hopkins questioned Elizabeth Clarke, an elderly and crippled neighbour who had been denounced as a witch. By the time Hopkins had finished with her she had named 31 others as accomplices. They were duly tried at the county town of Chelmsford and hanged. It was an impressive first effort. Thereafter he toured the eastern counties with a mission to rout witches wherever he went.

Hopkins was widely welcomed in his role as witch-finder. Norfolk county town King's Lynn paid him £15 for his services and Stowmarket a fat £23 – at a time when daily wages were as little as 2.5 pence. Doubtless, he cut a convincing figure. Fashionably clad in Puritan tunic and cloak, he boasted that he held 'the Devil's list of all English witches'. Like his European counterparts he ducked suspected witches into ponds and scrutinised

**Witchfinder General Matthew Hopkins preyed on elderly women, particularly those who kepts pets. During cruel interrogations they admitted witchcraft.**

their bodies for marks of the Devil. He was the master of the spring-loaded knife which fooled on-lookers into believing the victims really were witches. As Hopkins stabbed at the victim, the blade of the knife recoiled into the handle of the weapon, leaving the victim without a mark – clear evidence of sorcery.

Torture was illegal in Britain so Hopkins used his ingenuity. He subjected his victims to nightmarish terrors, without ever leaving a mark. Sleep deprivation was a favoured technique. John Lowes, a 70-year-old parson, was made to run around his cell without rest for three days. Guards were always present to make sure the ageing cleric did not sleep. Lowes was ultimately found guilty of witchcraft and sent to the gallows. Barred from having a clergyman read the burial service over his dead body Lowes recited it to himself before the noose was slipped around his neck.

Hopkins employed other tortures including starvation, solitary confinement and tying people cross-legged for days. His speciality was elderly women whom he found he could terrorise into submission with ease.

## A FIT OF SUPERSTITION

The last witch trial in England took place in 1712. In the dock was Jane Wenham, a 'wise woman' of Walkerne in Hertfordshire. Already under suspicion of casting spells, Wenham was thrown into jail after a young servant girl threw a fit in front of her. Wenham suffered the usual indignities of being stripped and searched for a Devil's mark. Under duress she named three other witches who were all hauled in but later released.

At Hertford Assizes the charge against her was 'conversing familiarly with the Devil in the form of a cat', no doubt a pet with which the lonely old woman consoled herself. Sixteen people gave evidence against her, including three clergymen. She was said to have a magic ointment made from dismem-

**THE LAST WITCH TRIAL IN ENGLAND WAS OF JANE WENHAM, A 'WISE WOMAN' ACCUSED OF CASTING SPELLS.**

bered corpses beneath her pillow and a cake made of feathers used for casting spells in her cottage. Wenham was found guilty and sentenced to death. Justice Powell, perhaps unconvinced by the valueless evidence, won her a reprieve, then a pardon.

After she was released the servant girl at the centre of the allegation against Wenham was found to be an epileptic and it was this condition that had caused her to convulse.

## FAMILIAR PETS

Women with pets were a prime target for the witch-finder as the animal was branded a familiar. Faith Mills, of Fressingham, Suffolk, admitted that her three pet birds, Tom, Robert and John, were in reality familiars who had wrought havoc by magically making a cow jump over a sty and breaking a cart. She was hanged.

For about 14 months Hopkins reigned supreme. Courtrooms and gullible juries were swayed by his damning evidence. When male witch Old Stranguidge was said to have flown over Great Shelford on a black dog tearing his trousers on a weather vane, the ripped garments were produced in evidence.

By 1646 questions were being asked about Hopkins and his motives. The hysteria which once accompanied his witch-finding activities was being replaced with distaste for the unremitting bloodshed. Cleric John Gaule wrote a pamphlet, *Select Cases of Conscience towards Witches and Witchcraft*, exposing the methods used by Hopkins.

About 400 were sent to the gallows by Hopkins in only 14 months. Sixty-eight people were hanged in Bury St Edmonds alone on his say-so and 19 people went to their deaths in a single day in Chelmsford. In England there are only 1,000 recorded cases of people being hung for witchcraft so the frenzy he engendered exacted a disproportionately shocking toll.

A wealthy man, Hopkins slipped back into obscurity at Manningtree. One legend says that he was himself accused of witchcraft but it is more likely he died in his bed of tuberculosis.

### The last execution of witches took place in:

Netherlands – 1610

Britain – 1684

America – 1692

Scotland – 1727

France – 1745

Germany – 1775

# THE HUNT

**George Jacobs was one of four men tried for witchcraft at Salem. Another, Rev George Burroughs, was said to have bitten young girls. After the jury peered into his mouth they were convinced of his guilt.**

Witch-hunting seized Scotland in much the same way as mainland Europe with persecution under both Protestant and Catholic rule. After Germany, Scotland vied with France for second place in the league of victims burned at the stake, these countries accounting for more than 10,000 between them.

James VI of Scotland, later crowned James I of England, inspired the witch panic, at least in part. He feared the power of witchcraft, firmly believing that a storm which lashed the ship bringing himself and his 15-year-old bride, Queen Anne, from Denmark was whipped up by occultists. Two women were burned at the stake – one while still alive – after admitting responsibility.

In 1597 he wrote *Daemonologie*, to counter Reginald Scot's sceptical book *Discoverie of Witchcraft* which appeared in 1583. The King went on to introduce harsh new laws against witches. James, a man whose hands were constantly black because he refused to wash them, was branded by France's Henry IV as 'the wisest fool in Christendom'. Yet he was enough of a scholar to study the legal cases brought against witches and grew to realise that many trials were unsound. He ended one of the most dubious forms of condemnation, that of denunciation by children at a time when the courts were prepared to accept any flight of fancy by impressionable children as evidence.

## SALEM AND THE END OF THE AMERICAN WITCH TRIAL

Children were at the heart of the famous witch-hunt in America at Salem in Massachusetts. In February 1692 a group of girls aged between nine and 20 visited the local minister's house to hear stories told by his Carib slave Tituba. Two of the youngest became hysterical and their symptoms were mimicked by other children. Word that they were bewitched spread through the rural community.

Under questioning, the children named three tormentors: Tituba, pipe-smoking Sarah Good and widow Sarah Osburne. Salem was in the grip of a strict Puritan rule. Was it a coincidence that Tituba was black and not a Puritan; that Sarah Good offended the Puritans by begging door to door and that Sarah Osburne had caused a scandal by living with her lover out of wedlock? None of the trio attended church.

Now the zeal of the witch-hunt rippled through the community and there were further denunciations. About 400 were arrested as the witch-hunt peaked while others fled the area to escape its tentacles. The accused who repented by naming other suspects lived. Anyone who continually denied the allegations of witchcraft laid against them ended up at the gallows.

The courtroom scenes in Salem were astonishing. Four men testified that bold, brassy inn-keeper Bridget Bishop haunted them at night, sometimes appearing with the body of a monkey, the feet of a cock and the face of a man. Her own husband was said to have thought her a witch. Other erstwhile respectable citizens were brought to court, apparently named by children during their convulsions.

The episode was sensational although the roll-call of victims was modest by European standards. Nineteen were hanged and one man was pressed to death after refusing to plead. By October the crisis was over. When the immensity of their actions dawned, the entire community repented. There was a day of public mourning as all involved struggled to understand what bizarre frenzy had enveloped them. The Rev John Hale, who gave evidence against Bridget Bishop, said: 'We walked in clouds and could not see our way.' The episode marked the end of witchcraft trials in America and no one was ever again pressed to death, so disgusted were the colonials with its barbarity.

## DENUNCIATION BY CHILDREN

Nine-year-old Jennet Device testified against her mother and 11-year-old sister in 1582 and both were hanged. There were scores of cases of children pointing the finger out of fear, wild imaginings or to cover pranks.

John Smith of Leicester feigned fits and the vomiting of pins to frame old women for casting a spell on him. Nine were already hanged on his evidence when James I intervened. At the King's behest, the boy was dispatched to the care of the Archbishop of Canterbury. Within weeks he broke down and confessed. No more would the words of children wield such deadly power.

**In his early years James I was a keen witch-hunter . . . later he realised many accusations were maliciously falsified.**

# TEARS OF WITCHES AND WOLVES

Medieval France was a hot-bed of witches and werewolves, according to witch-finder Henry Boguet. With an astonishing 30,000 cases reported in less than 100 years he created for himself an empire based on myth, menace and torture.

Boguet, Supreme Judge of the St Claude district in Burgundy and author of the French witch-hunters' bible *Discours des Sorciers*, was the country's most depraved inquisitor. Hundreds begged him for mercy, but their grovelling was to no avail. Moments later they found themselves in the hands of his steel-hearted torturers.

French law provided the merciless Boguet with a huge range of horrific tortures and punishments which he employed to the full. The wheel which splintered bones and tore sinews, the rack, branding, whipping, crucifixion, and the practice of crudely tearing at the flesh with white-hot pincers all had their place in his agenda. Cremation, and therefore burning at the stake, was known to be a reliable way to rid the earthly world of witches and werewolves. That was the fate for those who confessed to, or were convicted of, sorcery.

While dispensing such violence, Boguet was all the while looking for tears from his suspects. He believed werewolves were sorcerers and he knew with certainty that sorcerers could shed no more than three tears from their right eye. Boguet kept phials to hand in which to measure the tears of his victims. But in their terror, many victims found their tear ducts stayed dry. The ordeal was not over even for those who cried buckets might yet be tortured.

Boguet was not above disposing of the vital tears with the slip of a hand and resuming the agonising programme. With trembling lips his victims would confess to anything to escape his clutches.

## THE TEAR PHILOSOPHY

In his book, Boguet extolled the virtues of the tear theory. He wrote: 'The doctors esteem it one of the strongest presumptions that exist as a test of the crime of sorcery. I wish to report what has come to my knowledge. All the sorcerers whom I have examined in quality of Judge have never shed tears in my presence: or, indeed, if they have shed them it has been so parsimoniously that no notice was taken of them. I say this with regard to those who seemed to weep, but I doubt if their tears were not feigned. I am at least well assured that those tears were wrung from them with the greatest efforts. This was shown by the efforts which the accused made to weep, and by the small number of tears which they shed.

'Yet if I spoke to them in private they shed tears and wept with all possible vehemence. The same happened when they confessed. They then showed themselves more lively and joyous than they had previously been, as if they had been delivered from a great burden. Besides it is probable that sorcerers do not shed tears, since tears serve principally to penitents to wash away and cleanse their sins.

'Nevertheless, if you demand of sorcerers why they do not shed tears, they answer you that it is impossible for them to weep because they have the heart too much oppressed at seeing themselves disgraced by the imputation of a crime so detestable as that of sorcery.'

Among the hundreds who fell into Boguet's hands was one Claudia Gaillard who, according to witnesses, was seen to assume the form of a tail-less wolf as she transformed herself behind a bush. The triumphant judge recorded: 'Common report was against her. No one ever saw her shed a single tear, whatever effort might be made to cause her to shed tears.' We can only guess at the unspeakable tortures Claudia suffered before she was finally burned at the stake.

**A witchfinder commits a suspect to a bag to be thrown into the river. If she drowns, she is innocent.**

**Imaginations across Europe came alive with tales of werewolves like this one ripping the throat from a man.**

## RABIES AND IMAGINATION

How are the scores of sightings of werewolves to be explained? Some can perhaps be attributed to rabies, a disease which turns its victims mad and produces some classic werewolf symptoms, such as a frothing mouth and uncontrolled fits of aggression. A proportion, too, can be explained away as people suffering from lycanthropia – a mental illness in which the patient believes he is turning into a werewolf. There were sadistic sex maniacs who would kill and leave all the hallmarks of a werewolf. The rest were surely the result of vivid imaginations of neighbours who were all-too-ready to share their baseless suspicions with Boguet and his henchmen.

## THE WEREWOLF OF CHALONS

One of the worst-ever lycanthropes was the Werewolf of Chalons, otherwise known as the Demon Tailor. He was arraigned in Paris on 14 December 1598 on murder charges which were so appalling that the court ordered all documents on the hearing to be destroyed. Even his real name has become lost in history.

## THE WEREWOLF'S BELT

Mass killer Peter Stube was brought to trial at Cologne in 1589. He had raped and murdered numerous times, claiming that he had a magic belt which turned him into a wolf. It was in his wolf form that these horrors were carried out, he declared. Stube was sentenced to having his skin torn off by red-hot pincers before being beheaded.

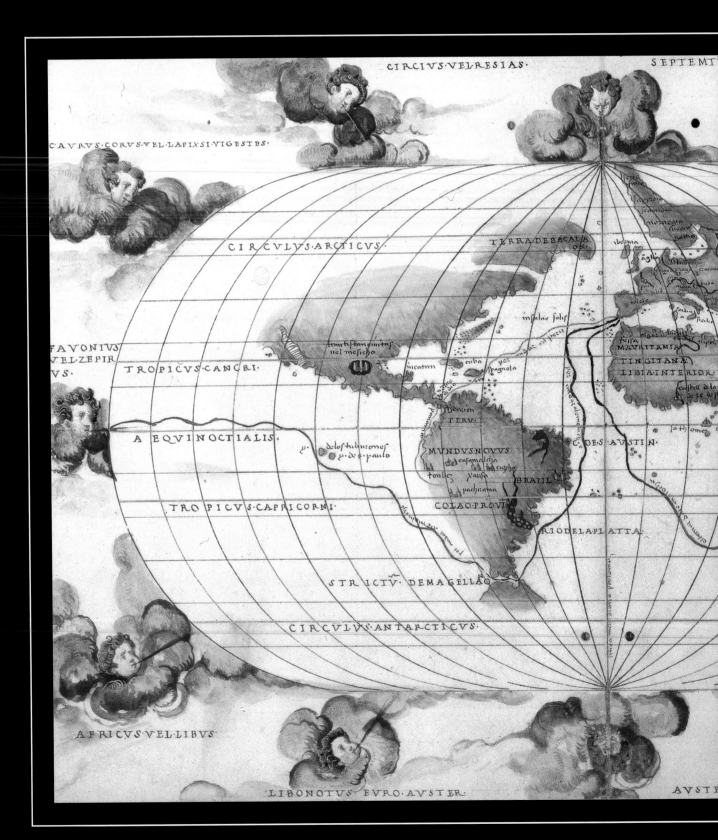

CIRCIVS·VEL·RESIAS·

SEPTEMT

CAVRVS·CORVS·VEL·LAPIXSI·VIGESTES·

CIRCVLVS·ARCTICVS·

TERRA·DE·BACALL·OS

FAVONIVS·VEL·ZEPIRVS·

TROPICVS·CANCRI·

MAVRITANIA·TINGITANA·

LIBIA·INTERIOR·

A·EQVINOCTIALIS·

MVNDVS·NOVVS·

C·DE·S·AVSTIN·

BRAZIL·

TRO·PICVS·CAPRICORNI·

COLAO·PROVI

IO·DE·LA·PLATTA·

STRICTV·DE·MAGELLAO·

CIRCVLVS·ANTARCTICVS·

AFRICVS·VEL·LIBVS·

LIBONOTVS·EVRO·AVSTER·

AVSTE

# BANISHMENT

Even in primitive societies, the threat of exile struck terror into people's hearts and minds. A savage punishment, it snatched men from their wives and children, so condemning even the innocent who were left behind to a precarious existence. And few who were banished survived the perils of isolation.

Yet out of this suffering a new world was born. Petty criminals were dispatched in their thousands to America and Australia. Against all odds, some felons became frontiersmen. Responding to the challenge of unconquered lands, they stayed, laboured hard and laid the foundations for affuent societies.

# A SOFT OPTION?

In ancient times, exile was much the same as a death sentence – but with an added *frisson*. The unfortunate victim banished forever from his home and community never knew when and how death would occur in the lawless rural outbacks. Lone travellers, universally loathed and distrusted, were easy prey. In Anglo-Saxon times the hunting and killing of those who had been banished was encouraged.

The exile of occasional troublesome sects or hardened convicts seemed too good an idea to waste. In 1579 plans were drawn up in Britain for galley fleets to rid the country of the bulk of its worst criminals. Naval personnel decided that galleys should remain the preserve of the French and Spanish, however, and expressed a preference for sails over oar-power.

Within 20 years the first law permitting transportation was confirmed. In the final years of Elizabeth I's reign, banishment went international. The destination for British convicts was America, discovered by Columbus in the previous century.

From the authorities' point of view, there was much in favour of transportation. Troublesome criminals were physically removed from Britain, so safeguarding society. The government was saved the expense of building new prisons to house the expanding convict population. By way of retribution, the convict had to endure an arduous Atlantic crossing, not to mention the back-breaking labours on plantations on his arrival.

**Above: Elizabethan ships were the best in the world. But the journey to the colonies still formed part of the punishment – many suffered sea sickness and scurvy en route.**

**Top: Settlers had a tough task on their hands as they tried to carve a living from the land. At first convict labour was valued. But plantation owners soon realised the quality of labour was poor.**

## JUDICIAL OPT-OUT

Here was an opt-out for the judiciary seeking a suitably stern penalty for those who arguably did not deserve the death penalty. Successive monarchs were delighted. They could magnanimously issue reprieves for those guilty of capital offences, replacing death with transportation, without appearing soft on criminals.

Yet there was a sizeable body of opposition. Some critics considered it a slight punishment, particularly for those convicts without homes and families. What purpose could this penalty serve when it left the criminal no worse off than he was before? Sometimes felons were hung for offences while others guilty of similar crimes received only transportation orders, so the system seemed bleakly unfair.

Many favoured swapping those due to be transported with the Christian slaves held in North Africa by its Islamic rulers. Others questioned the wisdom of sending Britain's workers abroad when public works at home could benefit from their labours.

## THE HARDSHIP EASES

As time went on, the convict could find himself healthier and probably happier being transported than the law-abiding workers he left behind him. His family was cared for by the parish so was in no undue danger. When bigger, faster ships were built to cross the Atlantic, many of the horrors of the voyage were wiped out. Some ministers came to suspect that criminals actively sought the penalty to improve their lives.

Transportation was subject to severe disruption during times of war. The Seven Years War between 1756 and 1763 hampered the exile of hundreds of men and women. Another difficulty proved to be the reluctance of the settlers in America to have hardened criminals on their soil. They were unconvinced as to the quality of the labour. As early as 1723 the burghers of Virginia attempted to stop the transportation of British convicts although the attempt was rejected in London. Later, plantation owners found a much cheaper source of labour, the slaves shipped in from Africa. Even before the War of Independence, which began in 1775, convict labour from Britain was virtually obsolete.

## TRANSPORTATION TIMELINE

**1597** – Transportation begins
**1685** – Transportation of convicts to America wanes following hostility from colonialists
**1718** – A revival in transportation courtesy of an Act of Parliament
**1775** – Transportation to America stopped by War of Independence
**1776** – Criminals once liable for transportation given hard labour instead
**1786** – British government agree to establish a colony at Botany Bay, Australia
**1868** – Transportation ends

**African slaves proved a better investment for settlers, ahead of transportees. They were fitter, worked harder and were passive compared with England's petty criminals. Many Africans were enslaved by rival tribes and then sold on to traders at markets.**

## CONVICTS FOR SALE

After the 1717 Transportation Act the government paid merchant Jonathan Forward £3 (later £5) to transport convicts from London and the Home Counties. On arrival in America, Forward could 'sell' the labour of each convict for the duration of his sentence to the plantation owners of Virginia or Maryland for £10. For women the rate was about £8. With some 30,000 people being shipped across the Atlantic in the first half of the 18th century it was a lucrative trade with a turnover worth more than £350,000.

# FINDING THE WAY BACK

## WITH OVERSEAS TRADE

## INCREASING IT WAS NOW

## EASIER TO COME HOME

As the New World flourished, commercial shipping across the Atlantic multiplied manifold. For trade it was a triumph. In terms of punishment it was a disaster for now the transported convicts found it easier than ever to come home.

Transportation terms were for seven years, 14 years or for life. If a convict with a seven-year sentence returned before his time and was captured on home soil, the next penalty would be 14 years. Those who absconded a second time were hanged. The deterrent was there but, as usual, the threat of hanging had little effect.

### RETURN TICKETS

Jenny Diver, also known as Mary Young, was an accomplished pickpocket and confidence trickster. She had a pair of false arms and hands which lay upon an apparently pregnant bulge. Her real hands, concealed under the dress, went to work without being seen, stealing from the unsuspecting in huge quantities. Diver was the mistress of many great scams, but the law finally caught up with her and she was arrested and transported to Virginia.

Upon her arrival in America, Diver persuaded an admirer to pay her return fare to England. She jumped ship at Gravesend and continued to pursue a life of crime. Caught once more, she was transported for a second time. She returned home again and was arrested for the last time. In 1740 she was hanged.

The London-based Poulter gang were more fortunate than Jenny Diver. Transported to the New World in 1738, they booked their return passage as soon as they arrived in America. There was little that the authorities could do to stem the tide of premature returns, despite a law passed in 1721 which permitted a £40 reward for the capture of anyone who had returned illegally from America.

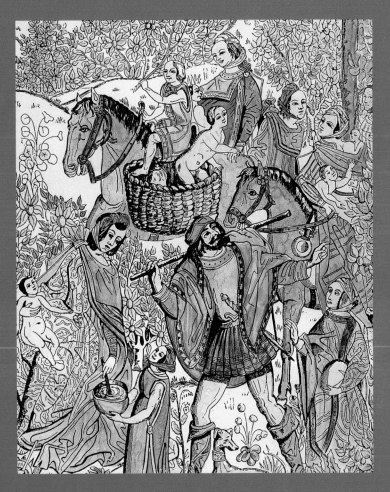

## GYPSIES

Down the centuries gypsies have long been persecuted and banished. Although the name is derived from 'Egyptians' it is thought the first gypsies came from India and travelled through the near east and North Africa to arrive in Europe in the 15th century. In England in the 18th century there were many attempts by the legislators to banish gypsies, all proving unsuccessful. There was widespread prejudice against them, however, and it was a punishable crime to be in the company of a gypsy. Prejudice continued into the 20th century as Hitler sought to wipe out gypsies, exterminating half a million in the death camps.

**Above: The skills of highway robbery were often learned from convicted highwaymen in the colonies. One highwayman who never had the chance to pass on his skills was Claude Dubal, pictured here at the scene of his crimes – Hounslow Heath. Shortly afterwards, he was arrested and hung.**

**Main picture: London's ports were bustling as traders and transportees set off for the New World.**

## CRIMINAL FINISHING SCHOOL

Another flaw in the system became evident over the years. There was nothing to indicate that a spell overseas would reform a deviant character. In fact, it seemed the opposite might be the case.

Petty criminal Henry Simms learned the techniques of successful highway robbery aboard his transport ship from fellow convicts. When he returned to Britain he put the theory into practice and terrorised travellers across the south-east before being caught and hanged in 1746.

It seems that the New World was something of a finishing school for those wishing to pursue a career in highway robbery. Highwayman William Field and his partner in crime were both transported to America during the 1760s. On their return they immediately resumed their occupation. Field was caught and hanged in 1773.

Stories of great lives of crime in Britain inevitably circulated among the white Americans, too. There's evidence that some returned from the New World to the old in order to establish themselves in villainy.

# THE TRIP TO
# BOTANY BAY

Diabolical conditions aboard the hulks, the floating prisons which took up the slack when transportation to America ended, forced Britain to rethink its penal policy.

The consensus was that Britain urgently needed another colony. First under consideration was the island of Lemane in the Gambia, West Africa. Its advantage was isolation. No guards would be needed to watch over the felons. But it would have amounted to signing the death warrant of the desperate souls abandoned there. Happily the scheme was dropped.

## CAPTAIN ARTHUR PHILLIP AND HIS BAND

Captain Arthur Phillip, a retired naval man aged 48, was put in charge of the first transport voyage to Australia. On arrival he would be governor of the colony. His fleet amounted to 11 ships, none of them large. Aboard were officers, seamen, marines, their wives and children and 736 male and female convicts.

Phillip was a conscientious man. Repeated attempts by the entrepreneurial transporter and the government to skimp on supplies enraged him. There was nothing aboard to combat scurvy, the dread sea-farers' disease. He wanted linen so the prisoners' rags could be replaced but got none. Fresh meat and vegetables arrived only at the last moment.

Another African venue, this time Das Volatas Bay in the south-west, became the favoured choice. But a survey commissioned in 1785 reported that it was a barren land. Without the opportunity to hack a living out of the soil the convicts would surely die. The only route now open to the government was the one that led to Botany Bay, on the Tasman Sea south of Sydney, Australia. The doubters comforted themselves that the opportunities for convicts to return home from this colony would be scarce.

### SHIPS IN PHILLIPS' FLEET:

**Naval warships**
*Sirius* and *Supply*

**Store ships**
*Borrowdale* (272 tons),
*Fishburn* (378 tons) and
*Golden Grove* (331 tons)

**Transports**
*Alexander* (452 tons), *Charlotte* (345 tons), *Friendship* (278 tons), *Lady Penrhyn* (338 tons), *Prince of Wales* (333 tons) and *Scarborough* (418 tons)

## THE PRISONERS' QUARTERS WERE IN DARKNESS. THERE WERE NO PORTHOLES AND LAMPS WERE BANNED.

## GAOL-FEVER

In February and March convicts rolled up at the Portsmouth docks to be stowed beneath the decks. The prisoners' quarters were in darkness. There were no portholes and lamps were banned. The only fresh air they enjoyed came via a hatchway – which was closed in bad weather. While the ships were within sight of shore the convicts were barred from the decks. It wasn't until 12 May 1787 that the fleet sailed, before which time 17 convicts had died in the gloom of the holds following an outbreak of gaol-fever.

First port of call was Tenerife on 3 June. After a week of loading supplies, the ships sailed for Rio de Janeiro. It took two searingly hot months to trek the Atlantic. Conditions below decks were intolerable with

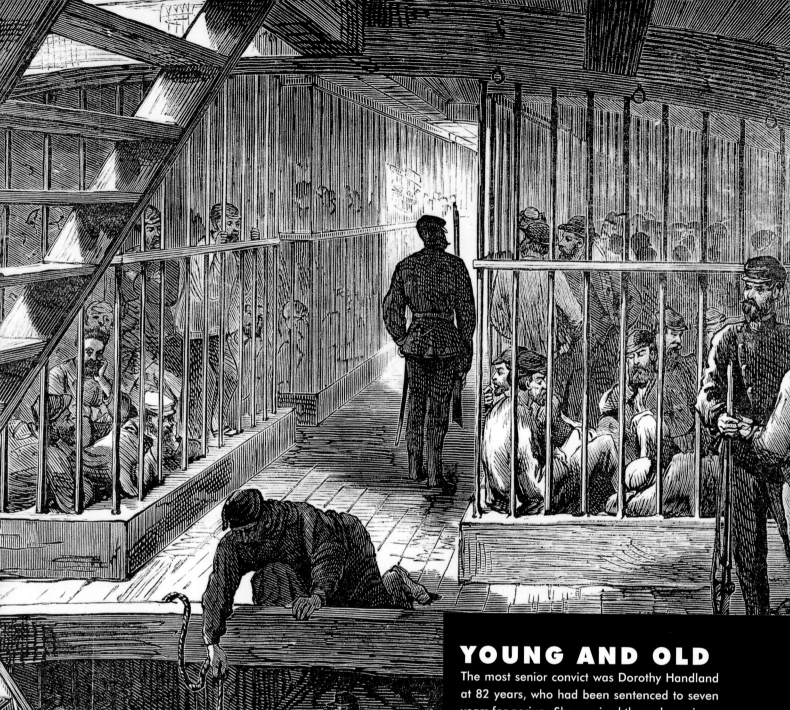

## YOUNG AND OLD

The most senior convict was Dorothy Handland at 82 years, who had been sentenced to seven years for perjury. She survived the arduous journey but hanged herself from a gum tree in 1789. The youngest convict was nine-year-old chimney sweep John Hudson, who had stolen some clothes and a gun.

effluent fouling the convicts' cramped accommodation. But at least they could exercise daily in the fresh air. The fleet then spent a month in Rio – which meant four weeks confined to quarters for the transportees.

Another six weeks at sea and the ships berthed in Cape Town, again spending a month in the colony. Taken on board were fresh supplies, also pigs, sheep, cows, horses and hens.

The last leg was the roughest with towering waves and storm squalls. They rounded Van Diemen's Land on 10 January 1788 and saw mainland Australia nine days later.

It had taken 252 days and there had been 48 fatalities of which 40 were convicts and five were their children.

**Above: At docksides prisoners on transportation ships were caged to prevent escapes. Ships were often in port for a month or more.**

**Right: The colony of Australia was formally founded by Captain Arthur Phillip on 26 Janaury 1788.**

THE TRIP TO BOTANY BAY

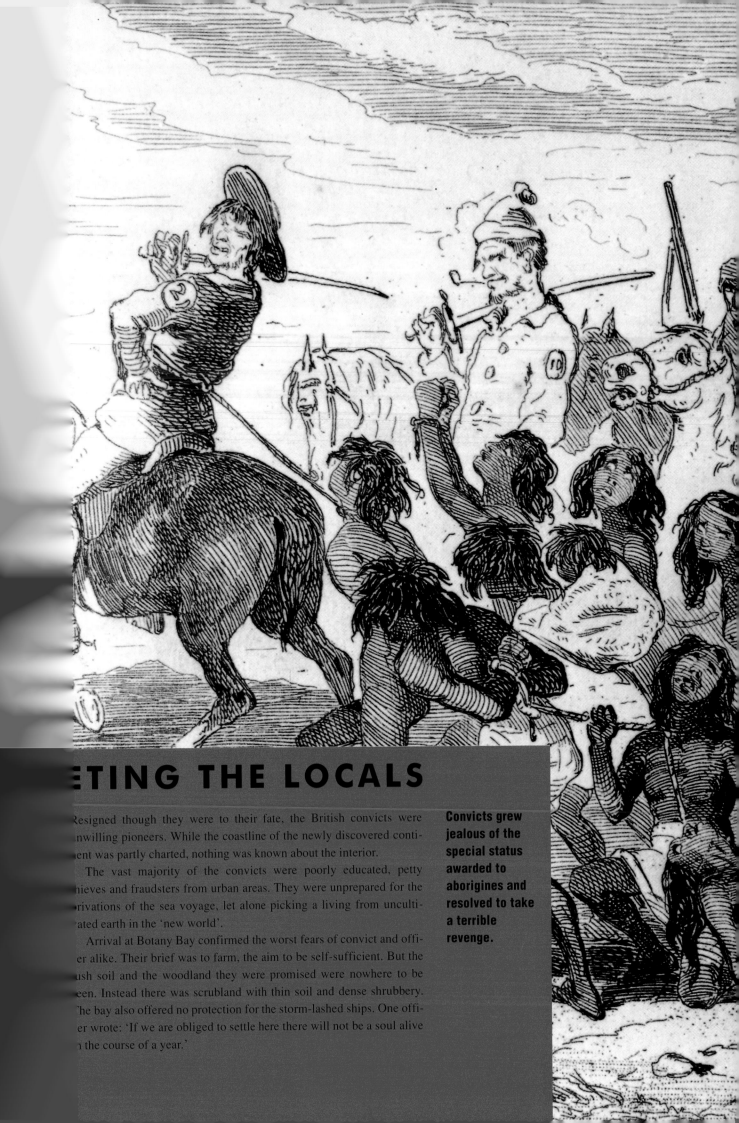

# ETING THE LOCALS

Resigned though they were to their fate, the British convicts were unwilling pioneers. While the coastline of the newly discovered continent was partly charted, nothing was known about the interior.

The vast majority of the convicts were poorly educated, petty thieves and fraudsters from urban areas. They were unprepared for the privations of the sea voyage, let alone picking a living from uncultivated earth in the 'new world'.

Arrival at Botany Bay confirmed the worst fears of convict and officer alike. Their brief was to farm, the aim to be self-sufficient. But the lush soil and the woodland they were promised were nowhere to be seen. Instead there was scrubland with thin soil and dense shrubbery. The bay also offered no protection for the storm-lashed ships. One officer wrote: 'If we are obliged to settle here there will not be a soul alive in the course of a year.'

**Convicts grew jealous of the special status awarded to aborigines and resolved to take a terrible revenge.**

## AN ALIEN LAND

Assessing the conditions as hopeless, Phillip and his fleet struck out north and came across Port Jackson, later known as Sydney Harbour. At least here there was a fresh supply of water and a fine natural harbour, although the difficulties of fruitless soil and clinging vegetation were still apparent.

Australia was an exotic new world. The sights, sounds, smells and weather were alien to the intrepid British. Clouds of budgerigars took to the skies when the intruders beat a path through the coastline. Vividly coloured parakeets and cockatoos joined them, squawking and screeching. There were bleating kangaroos, wallabies, possums, cute koalas and the curious duck-billed platypus. The British band arrived in the middle of the Australian summer and the glaring sun beat down day after day. For them it was as alien as life on Mars.

**Australia's wildlife was a sharp contrast to the fauna back home in England.**

## ABORIGINES

'Warra warra!' That was the cry of the native Australians as they emerged at Botany Bay on the arrival of Phillip and his ships. It meant 'go away'. To ram the message home, several aborigines treated the newcomers to a display of their spear-throwing abilities. The weapons flew some 40 yards, landing on the gravel with an ominous thud. There was no welcome for the white man from the aborigines. The aborigines' greeting would, no doubt, have unnerved the unarmed convicts.

In reply, a marine fired a blank cartridge over their heads and the natives fled. Soon they returned, intrigued to discover more about the uninvited visitors. Aborigines, who had lived for 20,000 years on the continent, were completely naked and were perplexed by the garb of the marines. When they prodded the breeches of one embarrassed marine Phillip ordered that the trousers be dropped. There was a responding whoop from the aborigines who perhaps feared they had been overrun by women.

### THEY ACCEPTED THE BEADS AND RIBBONS OFFERED BY THE BRITISH – BUT SPAT OUT THE WINE IN DISGUST.

The aborigines knew nothing of western culture. Even the sight of water boiling in a pot was a revelation. They accepted the beads and ribbons offered by the British – but spat out the wine in disgust.

A guardedly convivial atmosphere prevailed between the aborigines and the British. But little did the natives realise what was in store. For along with the fancy gifts the visitors brought cholera and 'flu, bugs which quickly claimed the lives of the unprepared locals.

Antipathy began to brew. Phillip was determined to appease the natives. Convicts and marines felt they had less status than the painted 'barbarians'. The whites, grew to despise the aborigines. Convicts pilfered their hand-made tools. In turn, the aborigines sought revenge by running through with spears the culprits they caught. Phillip forbade revenge attacks. It was a crisis that would worsen before it got better.

# KEEPING
# LAW
# AND
# ORDER

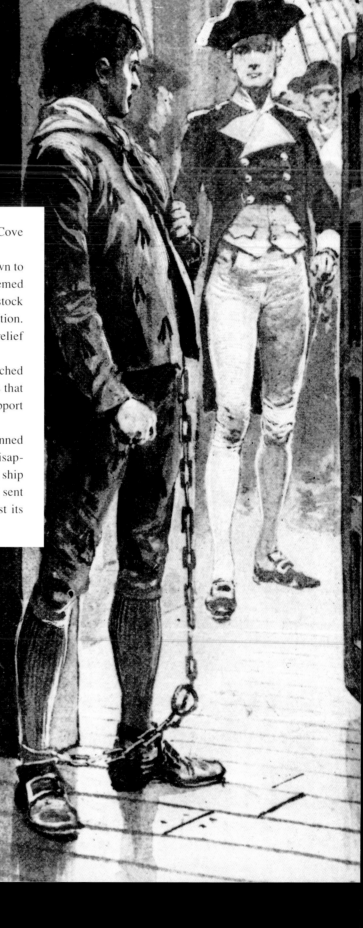

As the weeks and months wore on, the first settlers at Sydney Cove were ruled not by their hearts or their heads – but their bellies.

The ships had brought enough supplies en route at Cape Town to feed hungry mouths in New South Wales for two years. It seemed sufficient in those first days ashore. Apart from that, the livestock aboard the ships would breed and continue to feed the population. There would be crops to harvest and, in time, the bonus of relief ships from the mother country.

Yet the livestock was poached by convicts or died in the parched terrain. So unskilled at the basics of farming were the convicts that the sterile soil they half-heartedly hoed and raked could not support a crop. And the relief ships never came.

Day after day marines, their officers and the convicts scanned the horizons for signs of a sail. Month after month they were disappointed. It wasn't until 3 June 1790 that the *Lady Juliana*, lead ship of the second fleet, was spotted on course for Sydney. A ship sent from England in between times had struck an iceberg and lost its eagerly awaited cargo of supplies.

## A SECOND WAVE

At last there was news from home which the Britishers devoured as eagerly as the supply of flour. But now there were more mouths to feed as the fleet brought in new convicts. Convict and marine alike were already on the same starvation rations. This caused resentment among the troops who considered themselves worthy of more than the felons. Far-sighted Phillip realised that men and women were unable to work without food which is why he made the rations equal. He did not anticipate the disastrous effect on morale among the marines, who now sported threadbare uniforms and worn-out boots or bare feet.

The work carried out by the convicts was physically strenuous. Men were yoked like cattle in order to plough the fields. Unlike America where civilisation already existed, the convicts had to build every hut, office and shelter. Many died during their toil.

Punishments for stealing food were severe and were meted out to marine and convict alike. The lesser punishment for such an offence was flogging but the thieves risked being hanged. They were beyond caring. Famine fuddled their thinking and dominated every waking hour. Now the sole reason for living was to find food.

## DEAD ON ARRIVAL

Second fleet fatalities: more than 250 of the 1,000 men and women aboard the four ships of the second fleet perished at sea. The remainder were weak from disease.

Third fleet fatalities: one person in ten died as the third fleet sailed for the 'new world'. The rest, who arrived in 1791, were once again unfit for work.

**Opposite page: Although there was nowhere to run to, convicts on their way to Botany Bay were held in chains.**

**This page: Within a few short years the horizon at Botany Bay was decorated with an ever-growing number of masts belonging to British ships.**

## HARVEST AT LAST

The small vegetable patches tended by the convicts for the officers were beginning to show signs of success but it wasn't enough to supply the men, women and growing numbers of children that populated that bleak corner of Australia. It wasn't until 1792 that a substantial crop was brought in to feed the hungry troops and convicts. This was a moment of triumph. Governor Phillip returned home to England in December the same year, in the company of two aborigines, confident as he had been all along that the colony would finally thrive.

## MAKING A NEW HOME

Convicts on a seven-years term were eligible for a ticket of leave – the equivalent of parole – after four years. Those on a 14-year transportation term could get their ticket after six years, while lifers had to wait for eight. It was Phillip's intention to persuade some of these convicts to stay and work the colony. In 1792 he gave land grants to 53 freed convicts – although the vast majority saved their cash and bought a passage home.

# NORFOLK ISLAND

**Above: Convicts at work on Norfolk Island.**

A thousand miles east of Australia rising up from the Pacific swell is an island of the damned. Norfolk Island became a by-word for sadism, brutality and hopelessness when it was twice used to contain convicts considered too dangerous to remain in mainland Australia.

Governor Phillip had dispatched a second

## A THOUSAND MILES EAST OF AUSTRALIA RISING UP FROM THE PACIFIC SWELL IS AN ISLAND OF THE DAMNED. NORFOLK ISLAND BECAME A BY-WORD FOR SADISM, BRUTALITY AND HOPELESSNESS

lieutenant, Philip Gidley King, to settle on Norfolk Island soon after arriving in Australia. It was essential that the island was under British rule if the dream of having Australia as a major naval base was to be realised. King instituted a harsh regime where floggings were meted out for minor offences. His excesses paled, however, when his successor Major Joseph Foveaux got to work in 1800.

## A FLOGGING REGIME

Foveaux's appetite for the use of corporal punishment astonished even those who worked alongside him. One prisoner was lashed so often that his collar bones were bare of flesh and stood out 'like two ivory polished horns'. Foveaux attended the floggings wearing a smile of satisfaction. After being soaked by a bucket of sea water the victim was compelled to put his coat back on and resume work, which was usually breaking rocks for building projects.

Many other established penalties were made more horrific by Foveaux's terrible imagination. Leg irons were made smaller in order that they might cut into the flesh. The isolation cell was a subterranean water pit where its occupants dared not sleep in case they drowned. Women on the island were regularly raped by Foveaux and his men.

Foveaux left in 1804 having dragged the island to the depths. By 1810 it was decided to evacuate Norfolk Island and within four years it was once again deserted.

But Norfolk Island was left in tranquillity for just a decade. It once again entered the

Below: A flogging on Van Dieman's Land,
now Tasmania.
Right: A chain gang prepare for action
outside the Sydney Barracks.

equation of convicts and punishment when the British authorities sought a hell-hole for the most hardened of the transported convicts. The first to return arrived in June 1825. However, it wasn't until the new commandant, Lieutenant-Colonel James Morriset, was installed that the Norfolk Island nightmare began in earnest.

## LASHINGS AND CHAIN GANGS

Lashings were dished out by the hundred and were delivered with a specially made heavyweight 'cat'. Typically, they were staggered. So a man might endure 50 lashes one week and, just as his wounds were healing, 50 further lashes the next. The only treatment for men with their backs and buttocks cut to shreds came from nature – and it was an unpalatable one at that. Maggots attached themselves to the open wounds, gnawing away at infections. Flogging offences included insolence to officers, refusing to work, singing or even smiling.

Prisoners were laboured hard from dawn until dusk in chain gangs. Their accommodation in a wooden stockade was inadequate and they were plagued with vermin, most notably rats. Deprived of knives and forks, they ate like dogs.

**MORRISET EXERTED A SINISTER POWER OVER THE PRISONERS. HE BRED AN ATMOSPHERE OF DIVISIVE PARANOIA, BY ENCOURAGING INFORMERS TO DENOUNCE THEIR FELLOW CONVICTS.**

## THE END OF AN ERA

Just as Foveaux had discovered before him, there was no one on Norfolk Island but the powerless convicts to witness any brutality. Criticism only came about when visitors from Australia suspected gross maltreatment. Eventually the difficulty of overseeing the Island's regime became apparent and operations were closed down in 1855.

## MUTINY ON NORFOLK ISLAND

The harsh regime on Norfolk Island filled prisoners with resentment. But opportunities for escape were non-existent. Instead, convicts spent their time dreaming up ruses to alleviate their suffering. Some severed their toes with a hoe to win time in the hospital. Others poisoned themselves with berries. In truth, though, there was no place to hide on an island five miles long and three miles wide.

Still, the nagging lure of freedom occupied their minds. Predictably, their thoughts turned to mutiny. The mayhem that had threatened broke out on the morning of 15 January 1834. Prisoners turned on guards and released fellow convicts from their chains. Bold as the plot was, it was ill-fated. Shots at the start of the fray alerted guards all over the island. Armed and angry, they hunted down the mutineers and quelled the riot.

Ironically, it was the mutiny which helped to bring a measure of salvation for the convicts. There was retributive punishment from the Norfolk Island guards to endure which reduced the mutineers to human shells. But five months later, when Judge William Burton sailed to the island, the alarm bells began to sound in Sydney. Judge Burton was more impressed with the conduct of the prisoners than he was with the regime.

While 35 men were initially sentenced to death, Judge Burton immediately reprieved them until he could consult with the Australian government. Finally, just 14 were sentenced to hang. When they were told of their fate they thanked God for their deliverance. Those reprieved, wept anguished tears.

**79**

# DEVIL'S

**THE PRISONERS WERE TRANSPORTED TO 'ISLE DU DIABLE' IN STEEL CAGES IN THE HOLDS OF SHIPS. THERE WAS BARELY ENOUGH FOOD.**

As the British abhorrence for harsh penal colonies peaked so it dawned on the French that banishment was a valuable punishment.

In 1852 the first batch of French convicts arrived on Devil's Island, eight miles north-east of French Guiana, South America, in the South Caribbean Sea. These were the leper convicts who lived out their days in the tropical heat of the tiny jungle island. After 1895 physically healthy convicts were shipped there – in the knowledge that they would never return home to France again.

The prisoners were transported to 'Isle du Diable' in steel cages in the holds of ships. There was barely enough food and water to keep them alive. But worse was to follow.

## DISEASE AND CONFINEMENT

On the Island, the prisoners were kept in a wooden stockade. The Commandant and his men enjoyed the comforts of a government building. But much of the rest of the island, which measures just one square mile in area, was dense jungle.

With the jungle came disease. It was infested with alligators and flesh-hungry red ants. The surrounding seas were patrolled by man-eating sharks. Given that the chance of escape was slim, the penalty for runaways was the dreaded cells of St Joseph, nicknamed the 'dry guillotine'. This was solitary confinement at its most brutal, with no comforts and the minimum of nourishment.

One man, however, was determined to escape. Rene Belbenoit arrived on the island in 1921 and was horrified by what he saw. First he built a raft with a fellow convict. Undetected, they carried it through the jungle and all its horrors and set off over the sea. They reached Dutch Guiana – and were promptly dispatched back to Devil's Island by the angry colonial police. After 60 days in the dry guillotine Belbenoit could not stand and was so weak he could barely speak. But after recuperating he pledged to flee once more.

This time he constructed a canoe with the aid of eight other desperadoes. On Christmas Eve 1922 they slipped through the jungle and launched the rickety craft. This time they were stranded on the shoreline of a neighbouring island, chronically short of food and fresh water. Now the dry guillotine was judged too good for Belbenoit. For 80 days he suffered the privations of Camp Charvein, a malaria-ridden pit. When he emerged even the Commandant was awed by his spectacular stayingpower. With a few more failed escape attempts under his belt, Belbenoit became something of a celebrity.

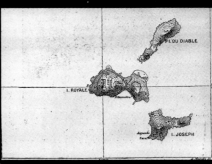

**Top: The guard room on Devil's Island overshadowed the prison hut which housed Dreyfus and his convict colleagues.**

## THE DREYFUS CASE

Captain Alfred Dreyfus was convicted of spying for Germany against his homeland, France, in 1894. Stripped of his army rank, he was dispatched to Devil's Island as a traitor to his country.

But suspicions that the disgraced Dreyfus was

# ISLAND

## FREEDOM AT LAST

When an American film producer visited the island to research prison conditions it was Belbenoit who showed him the ropes. Freedom was finally his when he and a group of comrades dug out a tree trunk to make a canoe and headed over water for British-held Trinidad. They stole away on 2 March 1935 and spent two desperate weeks afloat. Finally, they were washed up on a beach in Trinidad, some 700 miles from Devil's Island, and found shelter with the authorities.

Concern about the inhuman conditions on Devil's Island began to surface in France, much of it prompted by Belbenoit. In 1938 the penal settlement was shut down.

**Left: Alfred Dreyfus, the French army officer branded a spy, was dispatched to Devil's Island with hundreds of other convicts. The cell to which he was confined was spartan.**

**Top left: Convicts set sail for Devil's Island.**

a fall guy soon tore the country in two. Left-wingers were certain that the evidence against Dreyfus had been fabricated because he was Jewish and they agitated for his release. On the side of Dreyfus, among others, were the eminent writer Emile Zola and a clear-thinking army officer who found firm evidence that Dreyfus had not been a spy. Ranged against him, however, were the right-wing government and the majority of the French population.

By way of compromise, Dreyfus was pardoned for the crime he did not commit in 1899. He was released from Devil's Island, the only man to return home in the history of the sorry place. Finally, in a fresh inquiry in 1906 top-ranking army officials were exposed as liars, Dreyfus was belatedly cleared and France was greviously undermined.

# BANISHED TO SIBERIA

Banishment proved an irresistibly efficient means of punishment. Accordingly, it survived until the 20th century when it was most notoriously used in the USSR. The Soviet Union's most inhospitable region was ice-clad Siberia. So it was here that a system of gulags existed, the jails which housed those condemned to internal exile. Surrounded by barbed wire the gulags had a watchtower at each corner. On top of the towers were granite-faced guards with guns trained on the inmates.

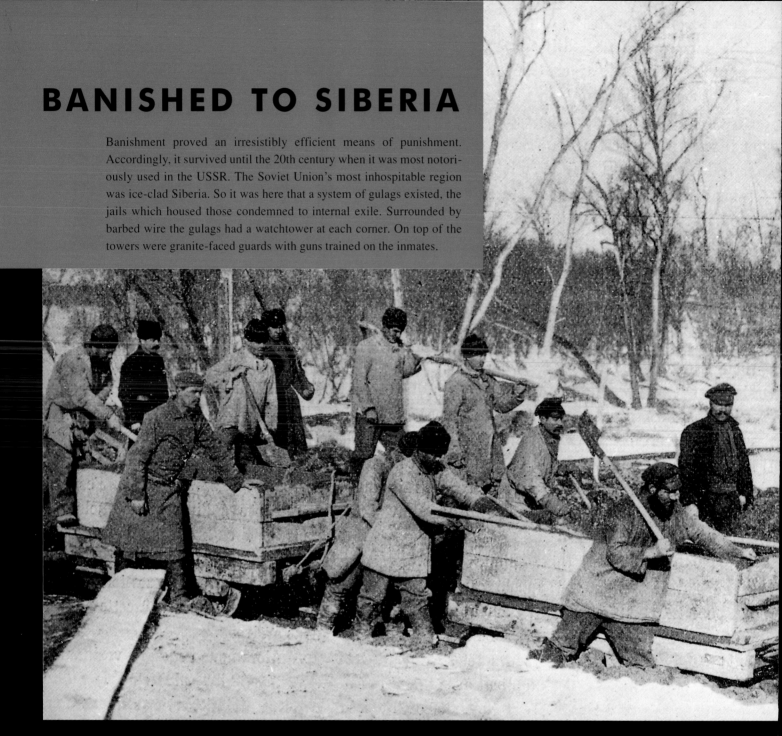

**Above: Gulag prisoners were forced to labour long and hard in inhospitable conditions. Yet food rations were poor.**

**Opposite page: Kulaks wave banners of protest after being deported from their village for defying Communist collectivisation policies.**

## TERRIFYING TRANSPORT

Gulags were as remote as any desert island. It could take months of travelling to reach them. Prisoners were transported there in crowded trucks towed by steam train. Up to 30 criminals were squeezed into a space designed for ten. Murderers, rapists, trades unionists, political activists and those persecuted on religious grounds – including Baptists and Jehovah's Witnesses – were sent to Siberia.

Conditions inside the wagons were at best spartan but deteriorated during extreme weather conditions. During a heat wave in 1972 several hundred prisoners, who had been all but abandoned by the guards, screamed at the tops of their voices when the train passed through towns and cities. Embarrassing the patrolling troops was the only way the prisoners could get much needed fresh air and water. As recently as 1979, 17 people died of suffocation in Kazan after a truck was left in the heat of the sun.

Inside the gulags, prisoners were issued with a uniform and a single blanket. No matter how cold the weather the ration of bedding was never increased. During the short, hot summer it was a punishable offence for a prisoner to remove any part of the uniform. Food was grossly inadequate with a daily diet of little more than rye bread, groats, cabbage and small quantities of rotten meat or fish. This was to sustain men and women who were labouring hard by day.

## THE KULAKS

Russia's feared tyrant Stalin used gulags to cage the Kulaks who were land-owning peasants blamed for the ills of Soviet farming production. Stalin was determined to drag the antiquated Russian rural economy into the modern age and chose to do it by a system of collectivisation. It meant state ownership of the land and its crops. Kulaks suffered endless misery and degradation. Their smallholdings were swallowed up by the state and five million of them were deported to the bleak northern regions of the country where they died in droves.

Along with them went many others who were not Kulaks but who opposed Stalin or had found the courage to speak out against collectivisation. One observer at the time noted: 'The best and hardest workers of the land are being taken away, with the misfits and the lazybones staying behind.'

The countryside was soon in chaos. Stalin used the food from the newly formed collectives to feed the powerful Red Army or hungry townspeople. Famine soon came to the countryside.

As food was shipped out of the countryside, the hungry peasants were tempted to hoard it or sabotage the transporters. In response Stalin began a series of show trials using trumped-up charges to deter the rebellious peasants. Children accused their parents of crimes against the state and fathers were found guilty of stealing food even when their families were starving. Those accused and found guilty were banished to Siberia.

As many as 20 million died in gulags. Many more perished on the land as part of Stalin's collectivisation plan. The disaster appeared lost on Stalin who said: 'One death is a tragedy, a million just statistics.'

## EXILED FROM IMPERIAL RUSSIA

Internal exile was a tool used by the Russian Tsars and Stalin himself was sent to Siberia before the October Revolution. However, security of the exiles was slack and reprisals for escape were tame. On 9 July 1903 Stalin was exiled without trial to Siberia, thousands of miles from his home. Within seven months he escaped with apparent ease. Stalin was exiled once again on 29 September 1908 following his arrest in March of that year. Police seized him for a third time on 23 March 1910. There followed short spells of exile and jail until he was released for the last time from a camp in the Arctic Circle in 1916.

**Stalin, the man responsible for more state-sponsored killings this century than Hitler, knew just how effective exile could be. Once in power, he plugged the escape routes.**

# PRISONS

Fortress, cage, dungeon or pit, prisons through the ages have been notoriously barbaric. Until the 18th century a society bent on revenge has cared not a jot if those held captive lived or died. The torment of convicts far outweighed the seriousness of their crimes.

Even modern history is marked by its cell hells, those nightmare penitentiaries which put humanity and compassion on the back burner in the pursuit of retribution.

# TOWER OF LONDON

Palace and prison, the Tower of London, perched on the banks of the River Thames, has long been a symbol of England's glorious past and glittering present. Yet it was the scene of some of history's most infamous deeds.

In the Tower of London a young king was killed along with his brother in one of England's most gripping murder mysteries. The king was Edward V, son of Edward IV and just 12 years old when he succeeded to the throne. His brother Richard, Duke of York, was aged 10.

On the death of their father, their uncle Richard, Duke of Gloucester, was appointed their protector. The young king had ruled for

77 days when his uncle had him confined to the Tower of London. Protesting that the king was lonely, the scheming Richard had the fretful Queen give up her second son to join his brother in June 1483. They were never seen alive again.

Claiming a plot, Richard then had prominent supporters of the young king summarily executed and had himself crowned in place of his nephew. The fate of the Princes was unknown – but widely guessed. There were frequent calls for them to be produced in the flesh and, in their absence, Richard was branded a murderer. In 1484 Richard was accused by the Speaker of the French States

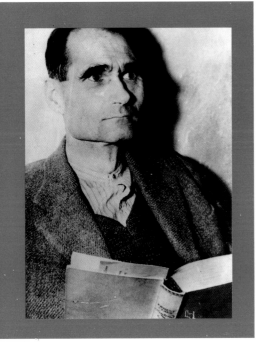

# THE TOWER– BRITAIN'S PREMIER PRISON

The Tower of London was built on a Roman site by William the Conqueror and was expanded and improved for years afterwards. This prestigious prison housed the high-born criminals of the day and was the home of the Mint, the Crown Jewels and other Royal regalia, a records office and an observatory. It was a zoo until 1834 and included lions, bears and wolves among its residents.

The last prisoner to be held there was Rudolph Hess, Hitler's deputy who fled the Nazi regime in 1941 in a crackpot bid to make peace with Britain.

**EXPLORER SIR WALTER RALEIGH WAS RESIDENT IN THE TOWER OF LONDON FOR SOME 13 YEARS BEFORE BEING EXECUTED OUT OF SPITE BY JAMES I.**

**Right: Were Edward V and his brother smothered by Richard's supporters, led by Sir James Tyrell? Tyrell was a descendant of the man believed to have shot King William II with an arrow.**

General Assembly of killing his brother's sons. The slaughter of children was a shocking crime and much of the population turned against him.

According to Sir Thomas More, the killers were Tower guard Miles Forest and a man called Dighton who together smothered the Princes in their beds. In 1674 two sets of bones tumbled from a wall in the Tower during repairs. Tests proved they belonged to two boys and it was widely believed they were the doomed Princes.

Intrigue still surrounds the case. Did Richard have his nephews murdered, risking public ire? Or was it a clever plan by Henry VII to oust Richard? One of the indelible marks the sorry affair left on England was the Tower's adopted name – the Bloody Tower.

Other inmates include Lady Jane Grey and her husband Guildford Dudley, whose scratched graffiti 'IANE' can still be seen on Beaufort Tower. Explorer Sir Walter Raleigh was resident in the Tower of London for some 13 years before being executed by James I.

Second division debtors and third-rate thieves, whose misdemeanours were too piffling to attract the death penalty, could find themselves thrown into jail. For centuries, that meant more, much more, than a mere loss of liberty.

From the Middle Ages to the 19th century, the prisons of Europe were as vile as any place that can be imagined. Indeed, the death penalty must have seemed merciful compared with the misery of existing day-to-day in prison. These man-made cell hells often amounted to a death sentence anyway as inmates perished by the thousand from disease, starvation and violence.

Prisoners were kept herded together in fetid cells which had no sanitary provisions, no heating and no bedding. They were manacled with irons, the heaviest of which weighed 40 lb, that left their bodies painfully contorted. By chaining prisoners together it reduced the

**IN 1759 *THE GENTLEMEN'S MAGAZINE* ESTIMATED THAT ONE IN FOUR PRISONERS DIED IN JAIL EACH YEAR, AMOUNTING TO SOME 5,000 FATALITIES.**

necessity for wardens and so saved money. At this time prisons were privately run, so profit, rather than reform was their primary aim.

The majority of the cells were underground with small slits or chinks the only access to daylight and fresh air. Meals, even clean water, were at a premium. Meat and bread, when it did appear, was served in great lumps, which the prisoners attacked like wild animals.

Soon parasites swarmed over inmates while vermin scavenged in the cells. The conditions were the same for those awaiting trial and for debtors. Flogging was a daily occurrence.

In Colchester jail, Quaker James Parnell was kept in a hole in the wall – like a baker's oven – some 12 feet (360 cm) off the ground. He reached the hole by climbing first a ladder, then a rope. After he fell from the rope he was bundled into a lower hole where he eventually died – although his demise took almost a year.

Another persecuted Quaker, Anne Audland, was held at Banbury in the 17th century in an underground cell with an open sewer running through it. The floor of the cell was covered with frogs and toads.

At Carlisle Castle 300 Scottish prisoners were crammed into one cell following the uprising led by Bonnie Prince Charlie in 1745. Scores of men were trampled to death overnight. In the same castle a dungeon devoid of daylight housed prisoners who were chained together by the neck. They found a single stone in the unlit dungeon which remained colder than the rest and sweated moisture. This stone became hollow by the weight of countless desperate tongues.

It wasn't only on the battlefield that supporters of Bonnie Prince Charlie were slain. Scores died after being captured and jailed, entirely because of the inhuman conditions of incarceration.

## A PRISONER'S LOT

In 1818 Quaker St Thomas Fowell Buxton described the lot of a prisoner awaiting trial. 'The moment he enters prison irons are hammered on to him; then he is cast into the midst of a compound of all that is disgusting and depraved. At night he is locked up in a narrow cell with perhaps half a dozen of the worst thieves in London, or as many vagrants, whose rags are alive and in actual motion with vermin; he may find himself in bed and in bodily contact, between a robber and a murderer, or between a man with a foul disease on one side and one with an infectious disorder on the other. He may spend his days deprived of free air and wholesome exercise . . He may be half starved for want of food and clothing and fuel . . .'

## GAOL FEVER

With sordid conditions such as these, disease was rife. Most notorious of all afflictions was gaol fever, an acute form of typhoid. Doctors stayed away from prisons where gaol fever was known to be flourishing. Reformer John Howard was horrified by the relentless outbreaks. 'From my own observations in 1771 and 1774, I was fully convinced that many more were destroyed by (gaol fever) than were put to death by all the public executions in the kingdom,' he wrote.

So deadly was the illness that everyone who attended an Assize held at Oxford Castle in 1577 was dead within 48 hours after coming into contact with a sufferer from a local prison. In 1750 the disease swept through the Old Bailey, claiming the lives of the Lord Mayor, two judges, an alderman, the jury and more than 50 others. It was taken into the courtroom by two convicts standing trial.

There was no gender segregation in the early prisons, leading to rampant promiscuity. Women actively sought to get pregnant so they could 'plead the belly' should they be

sentenced to hang. This meant that a death sentence could be commuted to a prison term or transportation.

When conditions in jails improved, prisoners would have their wives, children and even their pets installed. In England, it was not until 1792 that dogs were banned from the prison while pigs and poultry were allowed to

### IN GLOUCESTERSHIRE A REPORT OF 1783 ESTIMATED THAT THREE PRISONERS DIED OF GAOL FEVER FOR EVERY ONE EXECUTED.

reside within the walls of a prison until 1814.

As always, those with ready money did not face the same horrors. From the Middle Ages the rich were able to buy pardons from the King to short-circuit the system of punishment in Britain. Other wealthy prisoners in the ensuing centuries were able to purchase privileges which allowed them to live in relative comfort while incarcerated.

# THE COST OF CONFINEMENT

Much of the torment of the prisoners could be laid at the door of the wardens. Years ago men paid for the privilege of being a jail keeper – in 1728 the figure was £5,000 – and the pressure was on to recoup this enormous cost.

Squalid regimes were evident in jails up and down Britain in which extortion was the name of the game. Prisoners were charged admittance into jail. It cost the penned men to have manacles applied by the blacksmith – and taken off again. The heavier the manacle, the more expensive the 'easement of irons'.

Food and water were further expenses to be borne by the prisoner. Accordingly, the poorest might starve to death. When the day of release finally came another sum changed hands. In turn, prisoners turned on newcomers and demanded their cash, this income being called 'garnish'. It reflected the dog-eat-dog nature of prison life where the strongest ruled. Unfortunate new arrivals were stripped of their clothes and any other possessions they were foolish enough to bring with them.

Buildings fell into disrepair with some sections becoming uninhabitable, adding to the overcrowding of the prisoners, because keepers refused to part with the money needed for maintenance.

Prisoners who came to trial and were acquitted of the charges against them often found themselves back behind bars because of non-payment of gaoler's fees. Charges were levied by prison keepers until 1774 when an Act of Parliament outlawed them.

Some jails had grilles opening at pavement level on to the streets. Here the inmates would beg for money from passers by. Unscrupulous warders would happily charge members of the public to view the prisoners. Condemned men were the main attraction. While the 60 prisoners in Newgate jail's 15 murky condemned cells fought for a space to lay their head and pondered their doom, they grew accustomed to strangers peering at them through the gloom.

## WARDEN'S RULE

The wilful neglect of prisoners was cruel and frequently tantamount to murder. Attempts to bring wardens to justice were woefully ineffective, however. It was impossible to find a jury which would convict a man of mistreating prisoners. Prisoners were, by and large, feared and loathed in society. In 1728, three wardens stood before the courts in London accused of murder, robbery with violence and other crimes. When the jury acquitted them the judge refused to accept the verdicts. But a second indictment was likewise thrown out by the jury.

**Hungry prisoners clothed in rags begged at the grille of London's Fleet prison, dependent on the generosity of passers by to survive their term of incarceration.**

At Newgate prison the spectacle of condemned men during their last days and hours drew in crowds who paid handsomely for the privilege.

'SOME SINK AMIDST THEIR MISERY AND OTHERS SURVIVE ONLY TO PROPAGATE VILLAINY.'

DR SAMUEL JOHNSON ON THE BRITISH PENAL SYSTEM IN THE 18TH CENTURY.

## THE MAYOR'S CHAINS

A young Ludgate prisoner caught the eye of passer-by Dame Agnes Forster as he pleaded for money through the jail's grille. Intrigued, Dame Agnes paid £20 for his release and took him home to be her servant. In time the relationship grew sufficiently for them to wed. Now a respected citizen, Stephen Forster went on to become Lord Mayor of London in 1454. When he died, 10 years later, his widow paid for an extension to Ludgate jail to alleviate overcrowding, and financed a chapel and exercise yard. She also paid a sum into the jail so that prisoners would never again be charged for rooms and water. Sadly, the reform did not survive her.

## DEMOCRATIC DISASTER

In 1633 London's Court of Alderman ordered that the prisoners of Newgate elect their own wardens from the ranks of the prisoners. This bold experiment went disastrously wrong when the men, in reality picked by the warden, imposed an even harsher rule than ever. The 'partners' as they were called were guilty of stealing bread rations, confiscating gifts to prisoners and carrying out brutal punishments. By 1730 they were disbanded.

# DARK DAYS OF JUVENILE JUSTICE

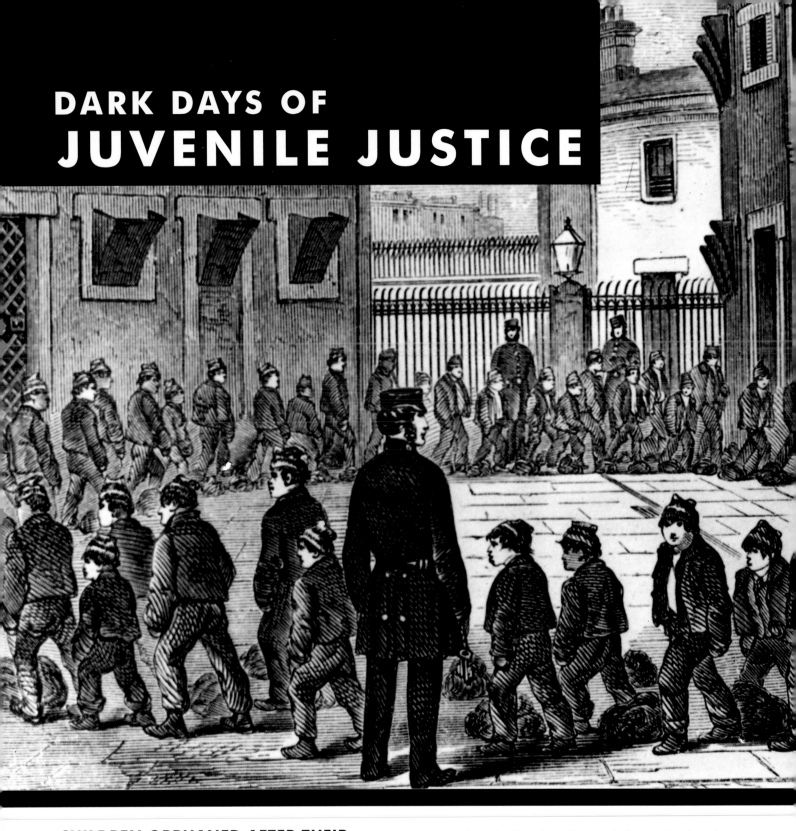

**CHILDREN ORPHANED AFTER THEIR PARENTS HANGED WERE SOON LURED INTO A LIFE OF CRIME. SOON MANY WERE THEMSELVES IN A CONDEMNED CELL.**

As a woman was hauled off to the gallows, a baby dangled from her breast and children clung tearfully to her skirts. It was a relatively common sight in the 17th and 18th centuries and one that should have melted the stoniest heart. But the judiciary remained unmoved, as did the majority of the people.

The family would have lived together in jail awaiting the execution day. And what happened to the orphans afterwards? They fell into the dubious care of the parish beadle. From there the youngsters were farmed out into the household service of those willing to employ new, cheap servant apprentices. A miserable life awaited them.

Mistresses like Elizabeth Hall were the rule rather than the exception. She used a rod to beat her two 'apprentice' girls, aged 11 and nine, every night. They worked from 4 am until 11 pm, very often with

## CHILDREN IN JAIL

There were also children in jail not because of their parents but on account of their own actions. Some juveniles even reached the gallows. As late as 1833 a nine-year-old boy was condemned to death at the Old Bailey for stealing goods worth twopence (less than 1p). He languished in the condemned cell of Newgate prison until a reprieve was subsequently issued.

Behind bars the juvenile prisoners shared the same hardships as the adults. Yet there was another burden to bear for they were bullied by warders and other prisoners alike. It is estimated that young offenders suffered twice the number of punishments dished out to the adults. A spell in jail would probably seal their future. For here was a seat of learning in the techniques of crime that would equip them for a life on the wrong side of the law.

Boys might find themselves behind bars for offences like stone-throwing or unlawfully knocking at doors. One boy was given 14 days in prison and a flogging for stealing six plums from an orchard. Perhaps the greatest scandal of all was that children were detained in the putrid conditions of the hulks (see page 96). One report made at the time notes 20 boys aged under 16 on the hulks, with the youngest being two years old! Many of the youngsters could barely dress themselves, let alone survive the rigours of this harsh environment.

Mothers who were transported were allowed to take their younger children – boys up to the age of eight and girls of 11. The fate of any older children was less than certain.

**Above: Mothers were able to care for their small infants in jail, while older children like those in Tothill Fields prison (left) were left to fend for themselves.**

## VICTORIAN DELINQUENTS

In 1862 the number of juveniles passing through British jails amounted to 11,749.

nothing more sustaining than a potato to eat. At the limit of their endurance, the children ran away and were found by the Watch – the police force of the day – in the street at 10 pm.

In 1796 a case was brought against Hall for cruelty. These were the days when servant-beaters were not considered as arch fiends and, had she killed them, it would have been unusual for her to be accused of murder. She was fined for her crimes and ordered to spend a year in a house of correction.

## SHADOW OF THE GALLOWS

A writer of 1833 declared: 'Nothing can be more absurd than the passing of sentences of death on boys under 14 years of age for petty offences. I have known five in one session in this awful situation; one for stealing a comb almost valueless, two for a child's sixpenny story book, another for a man's stick and the fifth for pawning his mother's shawl.'

The death sentences were commuted to transportation.

# PUNISHING THE
# POOR

Poverty came close to being a crime in 16th and 17th century England. Once the needy sought help from the monasteries but during the reign of Henry VIII most of these had been dissolved.

City dwellers feared the influx of penniless beggars from the countryside who were considered idle, lawless and a threat to the public order of the towns. Given their lack of work and inability to support themselves, it was thought discontent might breed among the poor resulting in social unrest or even revolution. The wealthy and worried determined to hide the poor behind closed doors. And so Houses of Correction or Bridewells were born, so called because the first was at Bridewell Palace in London.

Bridewell Palace was one of a number of palaces built by Henry VIII. Its dimensions were huge, with three substantial courtyards and scores of rooms. While foreign dignitaries occasionally stayed there, for most of the year it was left unused. Henry's son Edward VI decided to put some Christian theory into practice so, in 1550, he gave over Bridewell for relief of the poor.

**SIR FRANCIS BACON (LEFT), ARGUED THAT TO DETAIN THE POOR IN BRIDEWELL WAS AGAINST THE SPIRIT OF THE MAGNA CARTA.**

## PAYING THEIR WAY

The philanthropic gesture had its dark side, however. Those at Bridewell were made to work for the rewards of refuge, food and drink. Jobs included working the treadmills, beating hemp, making nails and even cleaning the sewers. Not only was the aim to improve the lot of the poor, it was to be self-financing too. Bridewell received its first induction in 1556.

Sir Francis Bacon, the eminent lawyer and philosopher, argued that to detain the poor in Bridewell was against the spirit of the Magna Carta, Britain's 13th century statement of civil rights. His objections were not heeded.

Most justices across Britain became keen to have their own houses of correction in which to dispatch the troublesome poor. By 1576 they were legally obliged to provide a Bridewell, as it became known, so the poor could be 'as straitly kept in diet as in work'. From 1609 the local

**Far left: At first the aim of the Bridewell was to house the destitute in clean, bright surroundings.**

**Above: As Bridewells gave way to workhouses in the Victorian era the poor were hopelessly exploited.**

justices faced a fine if they had not built one. At first those within a Bridewell benefitted in terms of diet, cleanliness and finance – they received a small wage. But it wasn't long before flogging was introduced to keep order among the inmates who, after all, had committed no crime. In the wake of the whip came stocks, and in some cases a ducking-stool. The labour became increasingly hard.

## THE POOR BECOME PRISONERS

Justices in Quarter Sessions, who had complete control of the Bridewells, soon seized on the opportunity to relieve the overcrowding in prisons and sent lesser offenders to the houses of correction. A criminal presence meant a prison regime had to be brought to bear. The defining lines between relief of the poor and the caging of criminals became hopelessly blurred and so persecuted Catholics and Puritans were detained with Spanish prisoners of war – alongside orphans and the destitute.

In 1682 the Governor of Wakefield House of Correction complained that 30 felons had been sent to him. In 1690 the number had risen to 67. When prisoners escaped from a prison or House of Correction, the governors faced a fine. So they were spurred on to make their institutions as secure and prison-like as they could afford.

The Bridewells were privately run. Eager entrepreneurs soon realised that their profits would be slight as the unskilled forced labour of the inmates yielded little cash. By the 19th century financial backing for Bridewells was scarce and the future of Bridewells and similar institutions was in doubt.

## WHIPPING UP A CROWD

Whippings at the Houses of Correction were a spectator sport. So popular were they at the original Bridewell that a gallery was built in the whipping room for the fee-paying voyeurs.

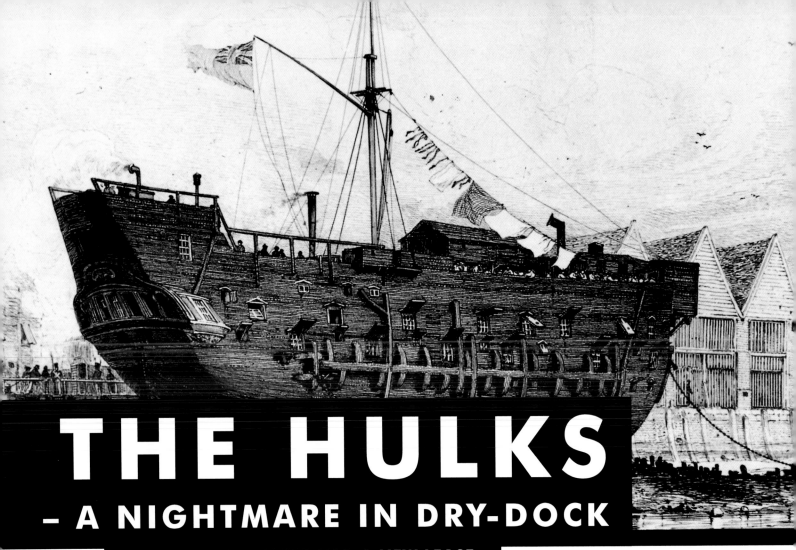

# THE HULKS
## – A NIGHTMARE IN DRY-DOCK

**BATTERED WAR SHIPS HAD A NEW LEASE OF LIFE – AS A GRIM PRISON FOR A GLUT OF CONVICTS.**

With the American Revolution came a headache on the homefront for the British government. The year was 1775 and the government had been happily ridding itself of a glut of convicts via transportation to North America. Now the arrangement had come to an abrupt end. The thousand or more prisoners due to be dispatched to the colony in 1776 were to stay in Britain. But where?

Jails were already chronically overcrowded and needed enlarging and renewing. It was then that the government decided to use old warships, called hulks, to contain the prisoners for a trial period until they could be transported to Australia. The trial lasted for almost 100 years. The introduction of the hulks heralded one of the most shameful eras of Britain's prison history.

An Act of Parliament passed in 1776 sanctioned the use of the first hulk and declared they were 'for the more severe and effectual punishment of atrocious and daring offenders'. Those words gave the red light for a brutal regime. During the day, life on the old ships was tough but not unbearable for the convicts. They were taken off the hulks and employed in dredging the river or constructing new dockyard areas. This was just what the government had in mind – as the benefits of forced labour were felt in the mother country instead of in some far-flung colony. By way of reward convicts received beer and, of course, filled their lungs with fresh air.

## DISCIPLINE AND DISEASE

At night the terrors began. The uniformed prisoners were loaded into the ship and clapped into irons. After that the hatches were battened down, committing the men inside to a dark, dank world of vermin, violence and intrigue.

The hulks were leaky and there was plenty of opportunity for rats to infiltrate below deck. In addition there were infestations of cockroaches, fleas and lice. Few alterations were made to the ships so the quarters were cramped and deeply unpleasant. Some of the prisoners were insane. Others engaged in further criminal activities, stealing and bullying from their fellow convicts. Wardens instilled discipline with the help of a whip.

Medical attention was minimal, disease rife. Given the insanitary conditions and the poor supply of fresh water it was hardly surprising that cholera and gaol-fever epidemics were frequent.

The hulks were sited first on the Thames in London, then on the Medway in Kent, on the south coast in Portsmouth, and to the west in Plymouth. Anything up

# AND POLICE

'Fleet Liberty'. That meant they were allowed day release – on payment of a sum to the prison keeper. Ultimately this was extended so a prisoner was able to escape the horrors of prison and abide in lodgings close by. The fee he paid to the prison keeper was for 'loss of earnings'. The area in which this occurred was known as the Liberty and it extended for a mile-and-a-half from the prison itself.

**Right: A lock-up full of petty criminals after a busy night. In the morning they faced the courts.**
**Below: For watchmen like these, the lantern was their greatest weapon. It caused thieves and robbers to flee.**

## THIEF-TAKERS

Without an organised police force the magistrates and judges had limited opportunity to capture villains. To improve the odds they offered rewards to gain informers. The reward system was based on the premise that 'every man had his price'. Sums on offer were high, with £40 being the norm for the capture of a highwayman. During the anti-royalist riots of 1795 a reward of £1,000 was posted for the 'discovery of any person endangering the safety of the Royal Person'.

Hand in hand with the reward system went free pardons. What better way to divide criminals than to turn one villain on his neighbour?

From the reward system came the thief-taker. Jonathan Wild, an artful 18th century crook, aimed to control the entire London underworld. He destroyed powerful gangs by bribing members to give evidence against others, claiming the credit for catching the betrayed men. Alternatively, he and his men would pounce on hostile gangs and hand them over to the authorities, again with a suitable number of witnesses.

He became a thief-taker *par excellence*, getting rich on the reward cash and enjoying the supremacy it gave him. Other criminal activities paved his way to the scaffold, however, and Wild was hanged on 25 May 1725. After his death there was a marked fall in the rate of convictions in London – and the number of hangings.

The reward system was open to other abuses, including the thief-taking of innocents. In 1756 Stephen MacDaniel arrested two men for robbing a tailor called James Salmon. Two witnesses testified against the pair, Peter Kelly and John Ellis, and both were hanged. Only later was it discovered that MacDaniel, Salmon and the two witnesses concocted the robbery story and framed the dead men.

Another scam was to stage a street robbery, complete with 'victim' and corrupt constable. A passer-by seeing the fray would help arrest the 'robber'. When they went before the magistrate the constable, robber and victim claimed the innocent man was the villain. The unlucky stranger went to the gallows as the real villains collected their reward.

# PRISON
# REFORM

## JOHN HOWARD

As High Sheriff of Bedfordshire, it was John Howard's brief to inspect the county jail. What he saw horrified him. He was concerned about the abuse of prisoners perpetuated by the wardens and the helplessness of the poorer inmates. It became his aim to see wardens paid fees for their services instead of stealing from the men in their charge. His campaign took him outside the county of Bedfordshire and into the rest of Britain. Howard's research culminated in *The State of Prisons*, a ground-breaking book, published in 1774, which gave remarkable insights into the appalling conditions that existed in 18th century English jails.

Howard, himself a prisoner of the French 20 years previously, had all the skills needed to sway the authorities. He was kind, firm, energetic and realistic. His concern about the prison system, and in particular the plight of debtors, became his life's work. It was his quest to improve the prison system which brought about his untimely death. Howard was inspecting prisons in Russia when he died in the Crimea of gaol fever in 1790, aged 64.

## MASKS AND VEILS

In addition men wore masks in jail to help preserve their isolation from fellow convicts. Women donned dark veils. Around their waists they wore tags displaying their cell numbers and it was by this impersonal code that they would be addressed.

The torture of silence and separation began to show in the mental deterioration of the prisoners. Solitary confinement was limited to new arrivals and then replaced by 'silent association' with other prisoners. Of course, as prisoners mixed, they would communicate in hushed tones and develop a sense of camaraderie. Ultimately, talking was allowed by way of reward for good behaviour. By the end of the 19th century pressure was exerted by the prison watchdogs to scrap the Rule of Silence. It wasn't reformed, however, until 1922.

John Howard did not live to see separation and silence imposed in jail. Had he witnessed its effects he would have undoubtedly reversed his thinking. Elizabeth Fry was one reformer who remained unconvinced about its benefits, even from the outset, stating: 'I do not believe that a despairing or stupefied state is suitable for salvation'.

## HOWARD'S LEGACY

John Howard (left) is still remembered today, thanks to Britain's Howard League for Penal Reform, which took his name. The campaigning group was formed in 1866 when it was called the Howard Association.

## SILENCE AND SEPARATION

It was the dream of 18th-century reformers to quell the hubbub that prevailed in prisons. How could a felon rehabilitate by contemplating his crimes when the noise all around him was deafening and distracting? During the commotion violence was rife and the innocent learned criminal ways. It was with the best intentions that they sought a rule of silence in prisons and for separation of prisoners. Like many noble sentiments, it was misguided.

John Howard, who sought single cells for prisoners, declared: 'Solitude and silence are favourable to reflection and may possibly lead to repentance.' Hardline clergymen also believed it was a sure way to have prisoners repent. Victorian jails were designed accordingly. Given that inmates faced a grinding daily toil – the 1778 National Penitentiary Act called for: 'Labour of the hardest and most servile kind in which drudgery is chiefly required' – the existence of prisoners became a painfully lonely one.

**Above left: A veiled female prisoner known to her warders only by the number on her belt.**

**Right: At Pentonville, as in other major prisons, men were masked and tagged for identification.**

**A CENTRAL OBSERVATION TOWER – FROM WHICH PRISON STAFF COULD OBSERVE ALL INMATES AT ALL TIMES – WAS TO BE SURROUNDED BY CELLS RADIATING OUT AND CONNECTED BY CORRIDORS.**

## JEREMY BENTHAM

Along with many of his contemporaries, the English utilitarian philosopher Jeremy Bentham was appalled by the system of punishment that operated in 18th century Europe. Inspired by a pamphlet written in 1764 by Italian nobleman Cesare Bonesana, Bentham became committed to the study of penology and in particular prison reform. In 1776 he published *A Fragment of Government* which contained the seeds of his ideas, and eleven years later his most important work *Panopticon or the Inspection House* appeared.

Bentham's penal theory was based on a revolutionary design for prison architecture – the Panoptican. A central observation tower – from which prison staff could observe all inmates at all times – was to be surrounded by cells radiating out and connected by corridors.

Goods manufactured by the prisoners could be sold to help running costs. Prisoners would receive wages, from which a sum was taken to provide a general compensation fund for victims of crime. While drink was banned, sex was to be permitted between male and female prisoners. Years ahead of his time, Bentham even envisaged hostels to provide half-way houses for prisoners.

Despite a government grant of £2,000 and the ploughing of £9,000 of his own money into the scheme, no Panopticon was ever built. His theories have since been criticised because he paid no heed to motive for crime, treating each convict the same.

Another of Bentham's ideas was the 'auto-ikon'. He wanted people to donate their bodies to science. After dissection, the skeletons would be preserved, complete with head, padded and dressed, so they could be publicly displayed. After his death in 1832, his corpse was made into an 'auto-ikon' and sits in University College, London – an institution which he helped to found.

**The design of a Panoptican: it was an inspiration for US penitentiary designers but was never built in Britain.**

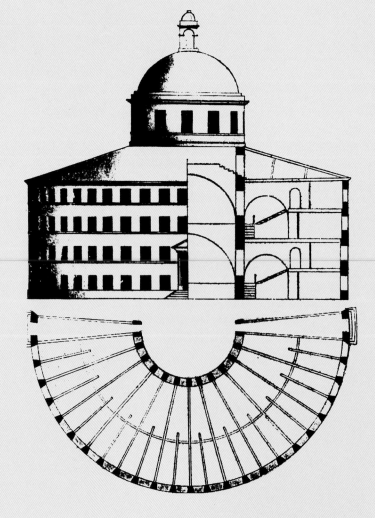

**THE AIR WAS SO FOUL
SHE COULD BARELY
BREATHE. SHE SAW
WOMEN WHO 'HAD
BEEN REDUCED TO THE
LEVEL OF WILD
BEASTS'. THE
INFIRMARY SHE
DESCRIBED AS 'THE
VERY BOTTOM OF
MISERY'S HELL'.**

# ELIZABETH FRY

When reformer Elizabeth Fry first entered Newgate Prison in 1813, she was shocked to the core by the appalling scenes, sounds and odours. The air was so foul she could barely breathe. She saw women who 'had been reduced to the level of wild beasts'. The infirmary she described as 'the very bottom of misery's hell'.

'In all my experience of filth, ignorance, vice, depravity and squalor, I had never seen its equal. The inmates fought, whined, begged me for money. I was heart-felt sorry for them – but my deepest pity was for their poor starveling (*sic*) babies, forced to sleep without proper clothing on the bare stone floor,' she wrote.

It sparked a crusade. She visited twice more to ensure that the children wore shirts and shoes and were given clean straw as bedding.

Elizabeth, a devout Quaker, had a strong constitution. But the abominations of the jail proved too much and prompted a breakdown. It was four years before Elizabeth, then aged 37, returned to Newgate to initiate a sewing room, school and some semblance of daily order in a newly segregated women's wing. A matron was appointed, ending the all-male hierarchy. Elizabeth formed the ponderously titled Association for the Improvement of the Females at Newgate which continued the good work. Meanwhile, she travelled the country, visiting every ship containing women prisoners bound for Australia. In 1838 she toured French jails at the invitation of King Louis Philippe and many of her recommendations were put into practice. Before her death in 1845 she had visited Belgium, Holland, Denmark and Prussia to prompt reform.

**Prison reformer Elizabeth Fry, pictured here reading the Bible behind bars, transformed the lives of women prisoners in Britain.**

# ALCATRAZ

An island named after a seabird and set in the bay of one of the most beautiful cities in the world, hardly seems the perfect location to hold dangerous criminals. But from 1934 until 1963 America's most menacing felons were imprisoned in such a location: Alcatraz Island in San Francisco bay.

Alcatraz, meaning gannet, became the site of a prison in 1868 when the US War Department decided to set up a high security prison for deserters and hostiles. By the 1930s the War Department's needs were surpassed by those of the Department of Justice, which was fighting a war against organised crime, and in 1934 Alcatraz became a federal prison under the wardenship of James A. Johnston. The first batch of prisoners to arrive at Alcatraz was the now notorious 'Atlanta Boys Convoy' which included Chicago gangster Al Capone. Special trains running to secret schedules were used to transport prisoners from all over the country to San Francisco, and very soon Alcatraz was home to more than 250 of the most dangerous criminals from all over America.

The prison operated a very tough regime with convicts locked up for more than 14 hours a day and banned from talking in the mess hall and the cell block. There was no system of special privileges, so good behaviour was not rewarded. Bad behaviour, on the other hand, was penalised: prisoners breaking any rule could be beaten with a gas stick, water hosed, placed in special handcuffs which tightened with every

## 'A PRIVATE PURGATORY WHERE CAREFULLY CHOSEN VICTIMS ARE SLOWLY DRIVEN MAD' – ALCATRAZ INMATE ON THE INFAMOUS 'HOLE'.

movement, put in a straight jacket or put in the 'hole' for an indefinite period and fed bread and water. The worst punishment of all was to be deprived of 'good time' – effectively time off for good conduct – since the federal system operated a scheme by which sentences could be reduced by ten days for every 30 days that a prisoner was well behaved.

Despite an impressive ratio of one warder to every three prisoners the excesses of this regime could not be maintained and within five years it had begun to weaken. However, Alcatraz remained the toughest prison in the US, a fact evidenced by the 1946 prisoner mutiny. A group of prisoners overpowered guards and stole their keys so that they could release prisoners in solitary confinement and open the prison's gun cage. During the two day siege, two prisoners were killed and afterwards three inmates were put on trial for their part in the siege.

By the 1950s Alcatraz had lost its unique reputation and was operating more or less like any other US prison, It was phased out in 1963, and the last prisoner, Alf Banks, left Alcatraz in June 1964.

Today, Alcatraz is a tourist attraction for the millions who visit San Francisco each year. But even now, with the prisoners and warders long gone, the cell room at Alcatraz retains a sinister aura that has undoubtedly deterred more than one wayward visitor from entering into the kind of criminal life that might lead to a term in a modern high security jail.

## AL CAPONE

Notorious gangster Al Capone was one of Alcatraz's most famous inmates. Capone's criminal career flourished in the 1920s when he became the most powerful man in Chicago's gangland, controlling a $5 million criminal empire. However, it was not until 1928 that the law finally caught up with him, and even then he was convicted of nothing more than tax evasion and sentenced to 11 years in jail. Capone spent five years in Alcatraz, arriving there in 1934 with the first prisoners from Atlanta. During his time in Alcatraz, Capone's mental state deteriorated as a result of syphilis, although the harsh regime may have contributed to his loss of sanity – a 1930s report suggested that 60% of Alcatraz inmates had become insane (gone 'stir crazy'). On his release Capone went into hiding, dying from syphilis in 1947.

**'GET BACK – ALL OF YOU! GET BACK IN YOUR CELLS! THERE'S GOING TO BE BLOODSHED!' – ROBERT F. STROUD (THE FAMOUS BIRDMAN OF ALCATRAZ).**

## TIME LINE

1860 a military prison for deserters and hostiles is established on Alcatraz Island.

1934 the Department of Justice takes over the military prison and converts it to a federal jail.

1946 two guards and three prisoners are killed and 15 badly injured as prisoners mutiny on the island. The siege lasts two days but is eventually resolved when Robert Stroud mediates between the prisoners and the governors.

1963 Alcatraz closes its doors to the criminal world.

**The cell room at Alcatraz was feared by even the hardest criminals. Convicts were locked up in silence for 14 hours a day.**

In a socialist 'Utopia' anybody who bucked the system was considered mad. That was the official view in the Soviet Union where dissidents were outlawed and punished. The authorities locked up those who rebelled, if not in a gulag then in a psychiatric hospital where they might be reformed into decent Soviet citizens.

The charges laid against those who objected to Soviet communism included 'mania for reconstructing society', 'reformist delusions' or 'nervous exhaustion brought on by a search for justice'. Anyone who committed an 'anti-social' act could find themselves dispatched to hospital for correction.

One Soviet psychiatrist made a chilling statement which highlighted the plight of the patients: 'The absence of symptoms of an illness cannot prove the absence of the illness itself.' In other words, medical evidence did not come into it. Dissenters would find themselves in a mental hospital whether they showed signs of madness or not.

Patients could be interred by a court, a civil procedure or on the word of a psychiatrist. Psychiatric hospitals were commonly housed in disused prisons, with bars conveniently at the windows and high security

measures already in place to prevent the inmates escaping.

Alongside those sent to asylums out of expediency were the criminally insane. By a quirk of injustice, those who were genuinely unbalanced, possibly psychopathic, were given jobs as orderlies. It is no surprise to learn that this power was greatly abused and that fellow inmates endured severe, sadistic beatings at their hands, sometimes with fatal results.

Drugs are routinely used in psychiatric hospitals and it is here that many torturous abuses occur. Potent tranquillisers like chlorpromazine and insulin were administered indiscriminately. Untrained or uncaring staff made sure injections were painfully given. High doses of certain drugs reduced the patients to living vegetables.

Dissidents might be held in psychiatric hospitals for periods of 15 or 20 years. Release was only secured when the patient displayed the correct attitude towards the Soviet Political system.

**Above: Horton Asylum in the Edwardian era. Many of the inmates were young girls who were sane until they were held captive for months or years on end.**

**Left: A committee established in Stalin's Soviet Union purged the country of dissidents, or objectors to the system. Some escaped the gulags only to find themselves in asylums.**

## YOUNG WOMEN WHO FOUND THEMSELVES PREGNANT WERE OFTEN CONFINED TO PSYCHIATRIC INSTITUTIONS BY WAY OF PUNISHMENT.

### RELIGIOUS RETRIBUTION

Religious dissenter Vasily Shipilov was arrested in 1939 for 'counter-revolutionary activities'. Ten years later he was declared mentally ill. In a psychiatric hospital he was given insulin, beatings and was regularly told: 'You'll be here until you renounce your religion – unless they kill you first.' He was a captive of the psychiatric system for 30 years.

### VICTORIAN VALUES

Soviet Russia was not alone in perverting the use of psychiatric hospitals. Britain's pious Victorians and Edwardians were appalled at illegitimate childbirth. Young women who found themselves pregnant were often confined to psychiatric institutions by way of moral punishment both before and after their baby's birth. Frequently the child was taken from them, inducing symptoms of grief. That was enough to keep them inside the hospital where the behaviour of other patients eroded their sanity. It was not unusual for these women to stay behind closed doors for the rest of their lives, forgotten by their immediate families and hidden from subsequent generations.

# CORPORAL PUNISHMENT

How much punishment can the human body take? In previous centuries this question tantalised the 'gentlemen' charged with disciplining the masses – men who were never themselves at the same risk of grievous physical abuse.

Corporal punishment was inflicted with relish, sometimes for personal gratification and always to show who was boss. Usually, it was inflicted publicly and the spectacle attracted large crowds, which heightened the humiliation. It was the age of the 'cat'.

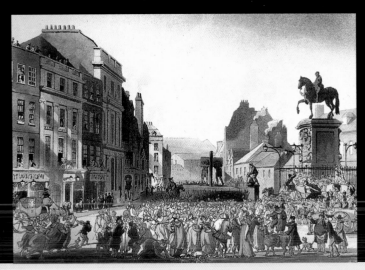

## THE STIGMA OF BEING PILLORIED WAS A POTENT ONE AND THE SHAME OF IT MARKED A SOCIAL CAREER FOR YEARS.

Alongside physical punishments, there were those penalties that inflicted mental anguish, namely the pillory and the stocks.

In a pillory, a man stood with his head and hands pinned by a wooden frame. Those who had erred more seriously might find themselves in stocks which had holes for feet and usually hands. That meant sitting immobilised and uncomfortable to face the crowd. Both contraptions were usually placed upon a platform. Pillories and stocks emerged in Britain in the 13th century and were exported to America with the Pilgrim Fathers. As punishments they were immensely popular with the authorities as they were cheap to administer.

In cases where the convicted man's crimes were not abhorrent to the masses, the crowd was sympathetic. Writer Daniel Defoe, author of *Robinson Crusoe*, was showered with flowers when he was pilloried for satirising the church in 1703. A man who was put in the frame at Cheapside for refusing to pay the government duty levied on soap in 1738 was cheered. Opponents of the unpopular Hanoverian kings who found themselves condemned to a spell in the pillory following outspoken attacks on the German royals were likewise hailed by the crowd – and sometimes even freed. This, however, was unusual.

Those convicted of unpalatable crimes could expect a torrid time. They would be the target of missiles like stones, dead animals, muck, rotten eggs and vegetables. The least they might expect was to become the captive congregation for a zealous minister who would sermonise at length on their misdemeanours. For this reason, sentences in the stocks and pillory were limited by the courts, even to as little as an hour.

Offences for which people were pilloried included gambling, perjury, prostitution, dishonest shopkeeping and low-grade frauds. Forgery was punishable by the pillory until the 18th century when it became a capital crime.

## PUBLIC OUTRAGE

Four men whose false evidence had helped convict two innocent men to hang were sentenced to an hour in the pillory in 1756. The charge against Stephen MacDaniel, James Salmon, John Berry and James Egan was a reduced one, that of fraudulently claiming rewards. Still, the crowd knew what the men were guilty of and were outraged.

MacDaniel and Berry endured their hour at Smithfield, suffering critical injuries from the oyster shells which were pelted at them. Three days later Egan was not so fortunate. An enormous stone had cracked against his skull during the first thirty minutes he spent in the pillory and he was dead before the constables came to release him. Salmon, who was beside him, was in poor shape. The three battered survivors of the pillory died from their injuries shortly afterwards in Newgate prison.

John Waller suffered a similar fate for the same crime in 1732. The crowd tore down the pillory and trampled Waller to death.

**Far left: The foot of the pillory at Charing Cross, London, was a popular meeting place.**

**Left: The stocks and whipping post on the green at Rutland are a sign of a by-gone age.**

**Below: Daniel Defoe had nothing to fear from the crowds. The words which earned him his punishment were popular sentiments.**

# HATRED OF SEX OFFENDERS

Sex offenders always incited a hostile response. Anne Marrow, a lesbian who dressed as a man and married three women, was put in the pillory at Charing Cross. Before she was released both her eyes had been put out.

Charles Hitchen was so terrified of the likely outcome of an hour in the pillory on a charge of attempted sodomy that he donned a suit of armour. He also bribed a sheriff to hold the crowd back with a blockade of carts. Within a matter of moments the athletic mob members had vaulted the obstacles in their path and were rending the armour and the clothes beneath from the hapless Hitchen. Only when the sheriff summoned reinforcements could his life be guaranteed. Frequently those guilty of sexual crimes only escaped with their lives because of the courage and determination of the constables.

In 1742 Thomas Lyell and Lawrence Sydney made £4,000 from gambling with loaded dice. They must have suspected their reception would not be a warm one and approached the pillory with trepidation. The sticks and stones hurled at them left them scarred and bloodied.

# FLOGGING

Whipping was a popular punishment for minor crimes. Thought by most to be harsh but fair, it was used from the Middle Ages to leave a mark, mentally and physically, on the erring classes. Gentlemen, however, were never whipped as the loss of honour was considered to be too great.

A flogging ordered by the courts would be carried out behind closed doors by the jailer in prison or, more commonly, in public by the hangman or constable. Given that the purpose of the punishment was to shame as well as to inflict physical pain the public display was deemed important.

The prisoner would be tied to the back of a cart, stripped to the waist and whipped while he was paraded around the town. Both the timing of the whipping and the route taken by the cart were chosen in order to attract the largest possible crowds. While army and navy chiefs specified the number of lashes, municipal

**THE POPULARITY OF FLOGGING ROSE AND WANED IN TURN. ITS USE PEAKED DURING THE 1770S WHEN IT WAS SEEN AS AN ACCEPTABLE ALTERNATIVE TO HANGING AND TRANSPORTATION.**

prisoners suffered as many strokes as could be administered during the route march.

Frequently a flogging was used in tandem with another punishment, like imprisonment. Although the anonymous author of the 18th century pamphlet *Hanging Not Punishment Enough* called for felons to be whipped to death, no fatalities were brought about during the progress of the punishment.

A variety of offences attracted the penalty. During the 18th century in Britain the theft of goods worth less than 12 pence carried the punishment of flogging.

In 1736 the gravedigger of St Dunstan's, Stepney, who sold bodies to a private surgeon, was sentenced to be whipped. Hangman John Hooper was wielding the whip. A huge crowd

gathered, including a mob of sailors and chimney sweeps, outraged at the foul crime. At the time it was abhorrent to have one's body dissected by the surgeons as it was thought to impede the passage to the afterlife.

After the wretch was bound to the cart they led the horses so slowly that he received hundreds of lashes. The hangman was given cash by the mob to take his time and do his duty most thoroughly, and was applauded as a hero for doing so.

Yet the memories of the mob members were surprisingly short. Only a few months before, the same hangman appeared at the Court of Aldermen to answer charges of selling the bodies of condemned criminals to private surgeons.

**THE DUAL PURPOSE OF FLOGGING WAS TO SHAME AND TO INFLICT PAIN SO IT WAS OFTEN CONDUCTED IN PUBLIC. STRIPPED TO THE WAIST, THE CRIMINAL WAS WHIPPED AS HE WAS PARADED THROUGH THE TOWN.**

## LENIENCY NOT ALLOWED

Age and infirmity were of little concern. In 1753 magistrate Mr Fettiplace Nott, of Lichfield, was confronted with an aged father and 15-year-old son who were guilty of burning the heath on Cannock Chase. He was reluctant to impose the recognised penalty of whipping and imprisonment with hard labour because he felt the father was too old to survive the ordeal and the son was merely following his father's instructions. Whipping would be, said Nott, 'an act of Barbarity rather than of correction.'

Both being first offenders, Nott ordered them to apologise to the steward who kept the land. The landowner, the Earl of Uxbridge, however, was furious. He instantly applied to the King's Bench to take action against the magistrate. Unable to finance his defence, Nott gave way and ordered the punishment should go ahead after all.

In 1790 Samuel Hinchcliffe was whipped after he posed as a porter at an inn to get tips from customers for implied 'future' services.

Women were whipped too, usually for 'keeping a disorderly house' or other offences related to prostitution. However, Mary Hamilton, who dressed as a man and married 14 women, was whipped through the town.

The popularity of flogging as a punishment rose and waned in turn during the 18th century. Transportation was frequently used in place of whipping after the Transportation Act of 1718. Instances of this corporal punishment rose again in the 1760s and 1770s as feelings against hanging and transportation ran high and an alternative penalty was sought. Yet before the 18th century was out, the number of floggings ordered by the courts had dropped once more, reflecting a public disquiet about harsh physical punishments.

**Opposite page: A non-conformist is lashed in London's Cheapside in an age of religious intolerance.**

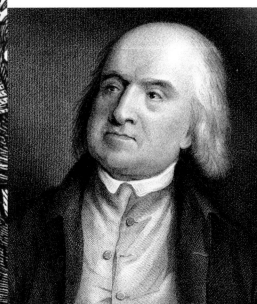

## PUNISHMENT FOR ALL CRIME?

Flogging was meted out for a broad range of offences. In 1772 two men were whipped around Covent Garden. One had seduced his niece, the other had stolen a bunch of radishes.

## THE HUMAN ELEMENT

A well-built, mean-minded executioner could inflict hideous injuries during a flogging while a smaller, drunken one might leave the victim comparatively untroubled. For this reason, prison reformer Jeremy Bentham (left) wanted to see a whipping machine introduced. He held that a machine with rotary flail could lash each offender with the same degree of force.

# ARMY DISCIPLINE

**ERRING SOLDIERS WERE COMPELLED TO 'KISS THE GUNNER'S DAUGHTER'. IN OTHER WORDS, THEY WERE ROPED TO A GUN AND FLOGGED.**

To most, military punishment can be summed up in one short ominous phrase – cat 'o nine tails. In fact, floggings did not enter the sphere of army discipline until the early 18th century. Before that, beatings were administered with sticks, birches or the flat side of sword blades.

Those who missed parade could expect to be put in irons while blasphemers had their tongues bored through. Of course, the death penalty existed in the military code set down in the 1689 Mutiny Act. Soldiers were hanged or shot if they mutinied, deserted, fraudulently enlisted, showed signs of cowardice or for a variety of other offences.

After flogging was introduced, it dominated. The 'cat' used for floggings was made from nine lengths of whipcord, about two feet in length, bound to a wooden handle. Each whip had up to nine knots.

Floggings were carried out during parades before the entire unit, by way of a deterrent. The prisoner was tied to a tripod to receive the punishment from one of the corps' drummers. After 25 strokes the drummer was relieved and a new man continued with vigour. A surgeon was on stand-by to intervene if the prisoner reached his level of endurance. The outstanding lashes would be held over for another day. Before the days of military courts an officer named the number of lashes in each sentence. A disgraced officer never found himself taking a whipping, he would be stripped of rank or cashiered instead.

## REPEATED DOSES

It was without doubt a distasteful business. In 1787 a surgeon, Dr Robert Hall, recorded the punishment of a soldier also called Hall who was sentenced to 500 lashes for house-breaking:

'He got 400 of them before he was taken down; and in the space of six weeks was judged able to sustain the remainder of his punishment as his back was entirely skinned over. The first 25 lashes of the second punishment tore the young flesh more than the first 400, the blood pouring at the same time in streams. By the time he got 75 his back was ten times more cut by the cats than with the former 400 – so that it was thought prudent to remit the remaining 25.'

Afterwards the prisoner said that the first 400 strokes seemed 'trifling' compared with the punishment carried out on the tender flesh which repaired the wounds of the first flogging.

Consider the plight of the guardsman who, in 1712 for the slaughter of his colonel's horse, was sentenced to seven separate floggings of 1,800 lashes each. After suffering the first 1,800, the remainder of his punishment was remitted.

For penning a controversial letter to a newspaper, 21-year-old Alexander Somerville, a private in the Scots Greys, was sentenced to 150 lashes in 1831. The ordeal made a deep impression. 'I felt an astounding sensation between the shoulders, under my neck, which went to my toe nails in one direction, my finger nails in another, and stung me to the heart as if a knife had gone through my body... He came on a second time and then I thought the former stroke was sweet and agreeable compared with that one.'

Somerville was whipped up and down his back and on his ribs. He was taken down after 100 lashes and spent eight days in hospital before returning to duties.

Drummers did not relish this work. One wrote: 'At the lowest calculation it was my disgusting duty to flog men at least three times a week. From this painful task there was no possibility of shrinking, with the certainty of a rattan over my own shoulders from the Drum-Major, or of my being sent to the black hole (a detention cell). By the time (the prisoner) had received 300 I have found my clothes all over blood from the knees to the crown of the head. Horrified by my disgusting appearance, I have, immediately after the parade, run into the barrack-room to escape from the observations of the soldiers and to rid my clothes and person of my comrade's blood.'

## HOW MANY STROKES?

Flogging became deeply entrenched in the psyche of soldiering. Indeed, the Duke of Wellington insisted it would be impossible to maintain adequate discipline without it. In 1834 a Royal Commission investigated the issue and came down firmly on the side of flogging although it favoured fewer lashes per sentence.

In 1807 King George III had limited floggings to 1,000 strokes. Less than 50 years later following the findings of the Commission and the death of a soldier widely thought to have been brought about by flogging, the maximum sentence was 50 strokes. The 'cat' was finally abolished in 1881.

## THE GLASSHOUSE

Military prisons first appeared in 1844, the largest of which was at Aldershot. After it was rebuilt in 1870 the three-storey cell block was given a glass roof and earned all army jails the nickname of 'glasshouses'.

## RIDING THE HORSE

In the British Army, soldiers accused of minor offences were sentenced to 'ride the wooden horse' (left). This condemned the man to perch on a wooden pinnacle with weights tied around his heels to exert maximum pressure on the crotch. Its only likeness to a horse was the mock head that was attached to the apparatus.

The piquet, or picket, was another eye-watering army punishment. The barefooted man was hanged from a post by the wrists with his feet in contact with sharpened wooden stakes in the ground. The temptation was to relieve the strain on his wrists by putting his feet down. Yet this was agonisingly painful too.

# NAVY DISCIPLINE

**ON AVERAGE, A FIFTH OF THE MEN ABOARD AN 18TH CENTURY BRITISH SHIP FOUND THEMSELVES ON PUNISHMENT DURING A VOYAGE – FOR MOST THIS MEANT A MEETING WITH THE 'CAT'.**

At sea, a captain was tyrant of his tub. To maintain discipline among the bold and bawdy men in his crew he used a variety of means, all of them painful.

The practice of 'starting', giving out informal beatings with a rattan rope, was an everyday occurrence in the navy. Far more serious was the punishment of running the gauntlet. This involved a man walking to the slow beat of the 'Rogue's March' at the tip of a sword, between two rows of his shipmates. The men were armed with 'knittles', small lengths of rope, which they used to beat him as he passed down the line.

A popular man who was loyal to his comrades might find the beating light. However, a man who had informed against other members of the crew was in for a rough time.

A mouthy matelot might be gagged by way of punishment, with a spike or splinter of wood bound across his open mouth.

Then there was 'grampussing', a punishment-cum-initiation ceremony at which a man's arms were tied above his head and water poured down his sleeves. The victim invariably exhaled sharply, sounding like a sea-mammal, the grampus, from which the practice gets its unlikely name.

**Above, left: Running the gauntlet was a viciously painful experience for men who were unpopular with the crew.**

**Left: The cat-o-nine-tails had at least three knots in each flail to increase the suffering of the victim.**

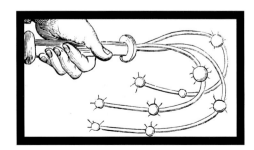

Captains could also confine a man to quarters, sometimes weighed down with irons, or more rarely impose fines.

Navy masters also relied on flogging to maintain order in much the same way as their army counterparts. However, the number of lashings per flogging was usually less than in the army.

On 4 January 1789 three men slipped away from Captain Bligh's ship *Bounty* before the famous mutiny and disappeared into Tahiti. When the runaways were finally tracked down Bligh showed commendable restraint in having two flogged with 24 lashes and one with 12, the penalty to be repeated again after a month. Bligh liked to have Tahitian tribesman present to observe the floggings, assuming it enhanced his image as an iron-fisted disciplinarian. In fact, they detested the sight.

On average, a fifth of the men aboard an 18th century British naval ship found themselves on punishment during a voyage – for most this meant a meeting with the 'cat'.

**Admiral John Byng was shot as he knelt on a silk cushion. But, was he guilty of cowardice or merely a government scapegoat?**

## AN OFFICER'S FATE

After Admiral John Byng was charged with cowardice, he knew that he faced a trial for his life.

Byng had been ordered to protect the British-held island of Minorca from the covetous French. Dithery by nature, Byng had 10 veteran vessels at his command while the enemy had 14 new ships. After arriving in the vicinity of the island, he delayed his attack giving the French a heaven-sent opportunity to regroup. The charge at the French line when it did come was badly planned and ill-fated. Byng, so far at the rear of the British force that he could barely hear the gun-fire, eventually decided to withdraw.

Back home, he was accused of 'lily-livered negligence' and arrested. At his trial General William Blakeney, the man forced to surrender Minorca, roundly blamed Byng. It was enough to condemn Byng to die.

On 14 March 1757 he was brought to the quarter deck of the *Monarch* where he tied a handkerchief over his eyes and knelt on a silk cushion before a firing squad.

Critics of the trial pointed out that Byng was nothing more than a scapegoat for the government, which should have sent a better-equipped task force to deal with the French menace. French writer Voltaire commented that Byng was killed 'to encourage others'.

# THE PUNISHMENT OF
# SLAVES

Abuse of slaves under the guise of punishment has long been a stain on the history of mankind. Slaves were particularly vulnerable to corporal punishment. Capital punishment was not an option as a slave was a valuable asset. Clearly, there was little benefit to a slave owner in killing his chattels – it had the same effect as destroying his own property. Incarceration was also ineffective in the punishment of slaves, as they had very little liberty to lose.

However, while the slave was on the one hand valued he was also reviled. The master happily employed a wide range of physical punishments to content himself that the slave was being kept in line. Slaves were particu-

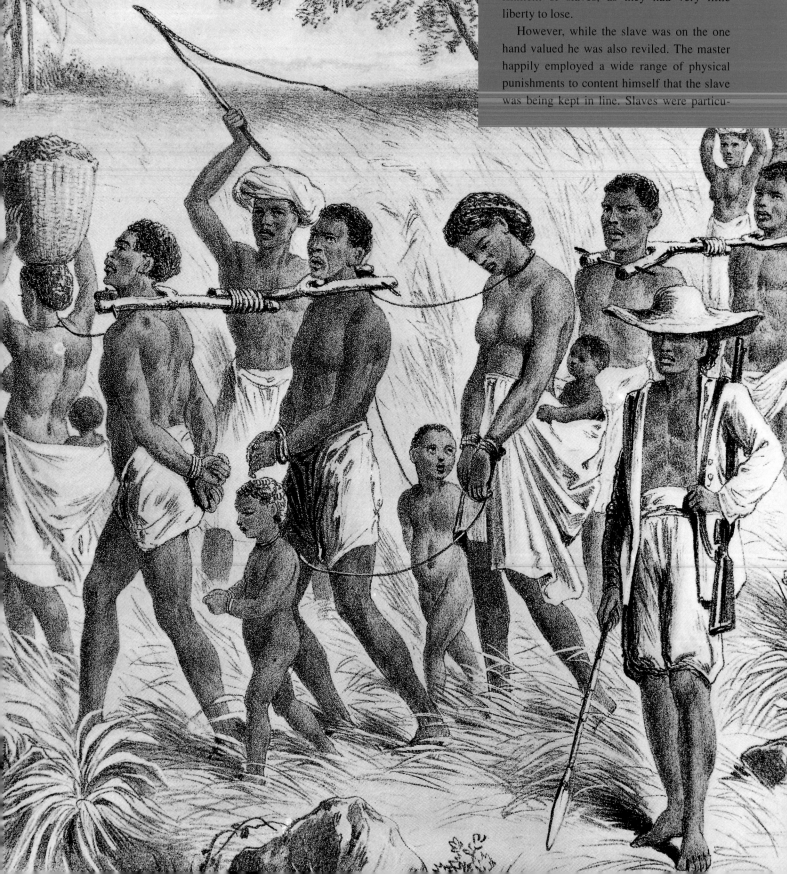

larly at risk when it came to sadistic owners who found a thrill in dominance.

No matter how they behaved, slaves were considered lazy, stupid, untruthful, untrustworthy and lusty. For these offences – mostly imagined – slaves were whipped.

During the 17th and 18th centuries, the mantle of slave punishment was taken up by the Americans. For a fee, a man could have his slave lashed at the neighbourhood jail by the local executioner. Anything up to 25 strokes could be delivered for so-called misdemeanours. It was essentially a private matter and did not need to go before the courts. Some slave owners even possessed their own whipping boards for use behind closed doors.

## WHIPPING WOMEN

Samuel Gridley Howe, a pioneer in the education of blind and disabled children, saw just such a punishment being delivered at a jail in New Orleans which he visited in 1846. He saw a black slave girl tied face down to a board with a waist strap securing her body. She was naked below the waist.

'By her side stood a huge Negro with a long whip which he applied with dreadful power and wonderful precision. Every stroke brought away a strip of skin which clung to the lash or fell quivering on the pavement, while the blood followed after it.'

The slave girl begged for mercy but to no avail. The flogging continued until her flesh became 'a livid and bloody mass of raw and quivering muscle.'

'It was with the greatest difficulty I refrained from springing upon the torturer and arresting his lash; but, alas! What could I do but turn aside to hide my tears for the sufferer and my blushes for humanity?'

Howe went on: 'This was a public and regularly organised prison; the punishment was one recognised and authorised by the law.'

Whippings like these were so commonplace they caused not a ripple of excitement from the inmates. Many prisoners could see, through their barred windows, the barbarity that was going on so close to them.

**Left: In Zanzibar, men, women and children captured or bought by the slave traders were yoked and then deported.**

**Right: Christian slaves in the 17th century were subject to torturous punishments at the hands of their barbarian owners.**

## CRUELTY IN THE CARIBBEAN

In the 17th and 18th centuries slaves were taken from Africa to work sugar plantations in the Caribbean. British plantation owners, deterred by the climate and disease, returned home and employed unscrupulous Europeans to run the business. Discipline was harsh, but overseers stopped short of killing slaves, who were considered a valuable commodity. Instead they ordered savage beatings which were not regulated by a system of law.

## SLAVES OUTSIDE THE LAW

There was no protection in law for the slave abused by his master in America's southern states. In South Carolina the law said that the slave was not 'within the peace of the state and therefore the peace of the state (was) not broken by an assault and battery on him.' Likewise, if a slave was attacked by anyone, he could not expect the felon to be punished for the assault.

If a slave died in the course of physical punishment, the owner simply claimed he had been in the process of 'correcting' the victim. Legal recourse against him was rare and even if it happened the most he would expect by way of punishment was the emancipation of his slaves or their forced sale.

Slaves were first brought to Virginia in 1619. With the cost of servants rising sharply, the use of slaves became commonplace by landowners for house and fields.

The production of tobacco was their first occupation in the New World until the cotton industry boomed in the late 18th century, which absorbed the labour of thousands of slaves. By 1850 nearly two thirds of all plantation slaves in the region were employed in the cotton fields.

An Act of 1807 banned the trade of slaves in America yet the culture of slavery still thrived in the southern states. The antipathy between North and South, with slavery as one of its root causes, finally erupted into civil war in 1861. When the North triumphed in 1865 slavery was finally abolished in the US.

Right: As they boarded ships to cross the Atlantic, people believed they were heading for a new life. But the system of punishments that evolved was in many ways worse than that of the mother country.

Opposite page: Quaker Humphrey Norton was silenced by Puritans in colonial America by having a key tied to his mouth.

## THE FOUNDING
# FATHERS

Although America was the New World the punishments meted out in the settlers' early days were reminiscent of the worst in old England.

Across the Atlantic went the pillory, stocks, the ducking stool and scold's bridle and the painful punishment of whipping at the cart's tail. Branding was as popular in America as it was in the mother country. Felons were indelibly marked with a hot iron. But the Founding Fathers were not content with established British punishments, so they derived new and ingenious methods of their own.

**ACROSS THE ATLANTIC WENT THE PILLORY, STOCKS, THE DUCKING STOOL AND SCOLD'S BRIDLE AND THE WHIPPING AT THE CART'S TAIL.**

## MADE IN AMERICA

There was the head-cage which was made of iron strips and moulded to the shape of a tulip. This curious contraption was placed on the shoulders of the criminal and encased the head to comic effect. Although it was weighty during the day, the device was little more than an inconvenience. At night it was a different story. No matter which way the poor victim positioned his head he was unable to rest, so contorted was his neck. Thus the punishment was not the wearing of the head cage but the sleep deprivation which ensued.

Given the religious zeal of the Puritan immigrants the advent of punishment by prayer was inevitable. As they sought repentance the criminals were compelled to kneel and pray on a tray of small, sharp pebbles.

There were sweat boxes, small sheds with an obvious purpose. Similar in design were lock-ups – the inexpensive isolation cells which caged prisoners in incredible discomfort. There was not room enough to lie or stand, so inmates were forced to squat until their sentence was at an end.

Cells were built in sewers to ensure that miscreants were confined in the very worst of conditions. Bread and water was the only sustenance prisoners received.

Prisoners were strung up by their fingers with their toes brushing the floor. Far worse was the punishment for sexual deviants. They were held on a rope by the genitals. Not only was the groin pain excrutiating but the stress on the back was unbearable.

## THE HOLY BOOK

The Puritans lived by the Bible and punished by the Bible. Community leaders interpreted the scriptures as vengeful and merciless. They developed a 'nanny complex', claiming that the pain they administered was for the good of the victim. Straight-faced Puritans declared that punisher was hurt more than the victim. In retrospect, many law enforcers were probably sadists who revelled in the agony of others.

Much later, in the 18th century, the tide of public opinion turned against the barbaric punishments meted out to criminals. Judges began to reflect the feelings of the people. Only in the southern states did relentlessly harsh punishments persist.

# CAPITAL
# PUNISHMENT

Death – the ultimate punishment – has long been a potent weapon in the judicial arsenal. But no matter how rulers have presented state killing, their principle motives have remained the same. Revenge and deterrence.

Countless thousands convicted of capital crimes down the ages have been tormented with the knowledge of the exact date and time of their impending death. Some deserved to suffer. But many were innocent . . .

# ROPE OR AXE?

**William the Conqueror**

A death sentence was bleak enough. But for many the personal disaster was compounded if the execution was to be carried out by rope. Hanging was thought to be good enough only for the masses. Loftier folk in Britain and Europe considered that they should be dealt with by the axe.

The nobility of death by beheading was instituted by the ancient Greeks and the Romans. As a means of punishment it was introduced from Europe into Britain by William the Conqueror. William was, in fact, opposed to capital punishment – until it came to his political opponents. The first man beheaded in Britain was the Earl of Northumberland in 1076. He was dispatched in the continental style by a swordsman. But the axe was quickly to become the favoured tool in Britain. The blood of Britain's finest families stained the axe down the ages.

## KEEPING ONE'S HEAD

If members of the gentry were sentenced to death by hanging they would throw themselves on the judge's mercy to switch the penalty to beheading. Not all were successful. In 1760 the fourth Earl Ferrers, who murdered his steward, was insulted when the court delivered its ultimate snub and his pleas for a punishment of decapitation instead of strangulation were rejected. Likewise, his request for a silk rope was also refused. Undaunted, he was taken to Tyburn gallows in a landau pulled by six horses, wearing a white wedding suit embroidered with silver – and was cheered every inch of the way.

**Left: Henry VIII ordered the deaths of the Countess of Salisbury, Thomas More and John Fisher when they refused to endorse his split with the Church of Rome.**

## A NOBLE TRADITION

For the next seven hundred years the number of capital punishments spiralled. Axing provided hordes of baying spectators with a gripping blood sport as scores of well connected criminals made their way to the scaffold. Just as France earned a reputation for beheading lords and ladies the same affliction blighted Britain, too. A French doctor travelling around Britain in the 16th century noted: 'In this country you will not meet with any great nobles whose relations have not had their heads cut off.'

Decapitations took place on a scaffold, a raised timber platform. There was a block upon which the victim could rest his or her neck. At first it was merely a chunk of wood. Later designs had a channel in which people would position their chins and necks. Many were high enough for the victim to kneel beside. The low blocks required the unfortunate criminal to lie down, a far more humiliating stance.

Axes varied in dimensions. The ceremonial axe once used for symbolic purposes at the trials of traitors and the like has a blade measuring one foot eight inches (50 cm) long and ten inches (25 cm) wide. It is secured to a wooden handle, five feet four inches (160 cm) long, which is decorated by four rows of brass nails. The axe is on show at the Tower of London. Most axes were similarly styled.

After the sentence was carried out it was customary for the executioner to raise the severed head before the crowd to prove the deed had been properly done. This was to prevent impostors from later staking a claim on the riches of the deceased by declaring they had miraculously cheated death.

## WARNING TO OTHERS

Death was not the only ignominy for the victims. Only a lucky few could retrieve the severed heads of their loved ones for burial. The head was generally taken from the scene, parboiled and then placed on a spike at a prominent venue to warn others against misdemeanour. For weeks, months and sometimes years the heads would peer down from that vantage point until they were dislodged by high winds, torrential rains or the need to make room for the new axeman's victim. In London the heads were lined up along the Southwark gatehouse of the 12th century London Bridge, a grim sight for travellers approaching from the south. Heads also decorated Temple Bar, which dissected Fleet Street, and Aldgate. Enterprising residents at these landmarks would hire out primitive binoculars to sightseers wishing to glimpse the mouldering heads of the famous – or infamous.

## AFTER YOU...

When two or more noblemen were to be executed at the same time, the most senior in title would go to the block first. In 1746 Lord Balmerino and Lord Kilmarnock were led to the scaffold. Every inch a gentlemen Lord Kilmarnock offered his friend first place at the block in order to spare him a grisly spectacle. So polite was Lord Balmerino that he declined.

Right: On the scaffold Charles I sent a final message to his people. 'And therefore, I tell you (and I pray God that I laid to your charge) that I'm a martyr of the people.'

Below: The death warrant which sealed the fate of Charles I.

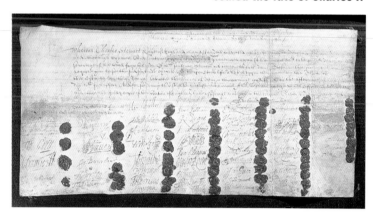

# A ROYAL BEHEADING

During the 16th and 17th centuries the block was stained with Royal blood. But, though many queens and lesser royals perished at the hands of the executioner, the only king to die on the block was Charles I. The Cavalier Charles ruled for 17 years before the outbreak of the Civil War. He had clashed with Parliament and attempted to rule without it. This fired the rebellion. Cromwell and his Roundhead forces routed the king before the Scottish army took him prisoner. He was handed over to Parliament in 1647 and stood trial at Westminster Hall accused and convicted of making war against his people.

A scaffold for his execution was built outside the Banqueting House, Whitehall. It featured one of the rarely used low blocks, calculated to insult his dignity.

Charles marched from St James's Palace to the sombre sound of beating drums on 30 January 1649, steadying himself on a gold cane. Flags fluttered in the winter wind but Charles was insulated from the chill by a blue silk vest, a doublet, gloves and a sweeping cloak. He carried four watches which he distributed to his closest supporters before his death.

Two executioners were in attendance, both heavily disguised for fear of retribution from Royalists. Dressed in black they wore masks, false beards and heavy coats to alter their shape. One of them was Richard Brandon, or 'Young Gregory' as he was known, and it was he who wielded the axe which beheaded King Charles. His assistant, who stood beside him on the scaffold was William Lowen.

## THE FINAL STRETCH

As he faced the executioners the King asked them not to deliver the fatal blow until he gave a sign. The signal was to be the stretching of his arms.

He tucked his tumbling locks beneath a white satin cap, with the aid of the executioner and an attendant bishop, and lay prone on the block. A devout man, he began to say prayers. The executioner was ready but Charles was not. 'Wait for the sign, wait for the sign!' he called. Moments later he spread his arms as agreed. The axe fell and Britain was without a monarch.

Thousands crowded at the scene. The atmosphere was far from gleeful, however, and most felt they were beholding a national disaster. One bystander was 17-year-old Philip Henry who wrote: 'The blow I saw given and can truly say with a sad heart at the instant whereof, I remember well, there was such a groan by the thousands then present as I never heard before and desire I may never hear again.'

## PASSING THE ROYAL SALT

In 1813 the coffin of Charles I was exhumed from a vault at St George's Chapel, Windsor, where it had been laid to rest. Sir Henry Halford accompanied the Prince Regent in viewing the remains. He cut off a lock of the dead king's hair which he later gave to the writer Sir Walter Scott and removed a verte-bra – which he used as a salt cellar on his dinner table. Only when a furious Queen Victoria heard of it some 30 years later was the section of backbone returned to the body.

## A SORRY DEATH

It is said Brandon was reluctant to take the life of a king and had to be brought to the scaffold by soldiers. By way of reward he was given £30 in half-crowns, an orange spiked with cloves and the king's handker-chief. Not long afterwards the executioner fell ill. He died on 20 June 1649 and many believed 'he died of remorse at killing a king'.

## STILL NO SON

With the divorce complete, the lovers wed just before the child arrived. To Henry's crashing disappointment it was another girl. The child was destined to achieve greatness as Elizabeth I – but Henry was furious. He claimed Anne had bewitched him, that she had an extra nipple with which to suckle a demon.

As he lost interest in Anne he alighted on the charms of Jane Seymour. After finding the King and Jane in bed together at Hampton Court, it is possible that Anne sought warmth elsewhere. At any rate, she was accused of adultery and sentenced to be burnt alive or beheaded. With a kindness perhaps invoked by their former passion, Henry agreed that the sentence could be carried out by sword so she was spared the agony of dying in flames.

On 19 May 1536 Anne was paraded through the crowds from her prison in the Tower of London to a five-feet-high scaffold constructed on Tower Green. It was made purposefully prominent so that everyone could see the execution. Her dark hair was hidden beneath a close fitting cap. White ermine fur lined the grey cape that she wore and a crucifix dangled from the belt of a crimson skirt. She carried a handkerchief and a small, gold-bound prayer book.

## A SINGLE BLOW

There was time for Anne to pray and to make a short speech during which she spoke of her innocence and loyalty to the King before she was blindfolded. Now the headsman pulled his hefty sword from beneath the straw on the platform. While Anne was distracted by the sound of movement from his assistant, he struck a single blow.

The executioner was paid 100 crowns, a considerable sum. As for Henry, he was engaged to Jane Seymour the day after the execution and married to her a week later.

**Right: Anne Boleyn just prior to her execution.**

**Below: Catherine Howard – executed in 1542.**

**HENRY VIII WAS A GREAT BELIEVER IN CAPITAL PUNISHMENT. IT IS ESTIMATED THAT DURING HIS 38-YEAR REIGN ABOUT 72,000 PEOPLE WERE EXECUTED.**

## ANOTHER QUEEN'S HEAD

Catherine Howard, 20, married Henry VIII in 1540, his fifth wife and the second who would lose her head. Within two years Henry was weary of her and all too ready to believe the gossips at court who accused her of infidelity. When she was seized by the guards at Hampton Court Palace she fought them off in a bid to confront her husband. He was at Mass and refused to see his distressed wife. It is here that her screaming ghost is said to wander.

Showing commendable calm the doomed Queen called for the block to be brought to her cell on the eve of her execution. With perplexed officers of the Tower looking on she knelt down to try the block for size. She died on 15 February 1542 along with her lady-in-waiting, Lady Rochford.

Mary was the Catholic Queen of Scotland. Elizabeth I was the protestant Queen of England. Given the long running spat between the two countries and their opposing religions, the realms were destined to collide.

Mary was the daughter of James V of Scotland and the French noblewoman, Mary of Guise. She was also a great-niece of Henry VIII which gave her a claim on the English throne. Mary had grown up in France and married the heir to the French throne, Francis. After his death in 1561 she returned to Scotland and wed her cousin, Lord Darnley. Six years later he was murdered and she married again. This time her groom was Bothwell, the man thought to be Darnley's killer.

# MARY QUEEN

## DEATH SENTENCE

Scotland was divided in its support between Mary and her son, James (who later became James I, England's first Stuart King). Mary was ultimately exiled from Scotland and fled to England where she posed a threat to Queen Elizabeth I. If Mary herself did not aim to harm the Queen, she became the focus of plots against the monarch. Accordingly, she was convicted of treason and sentenced to death.

The execution took place in 1587, in the Great Hall of Fotheringhay Castle, near Peterborough. When the executioners asked

**The spat between Catholics and Protestants was behind Mary's execution for treason.**

AS A GREAT NIECE OF HENRY VIII, MARY HAD A

THREE
BLOODY SWINGS

## CATCH ME IF YOU CAN

Margaret Pole, the Countess of Salisbury, proved hard labour for the executioner. She was the mother of Cardinal Pole who fell out with Henry VIII over his divorce. The King sought revenge against the entire family and imprisoned the ageing Countess in the Tower of London for two years, denying her essential creature comforts or a trial. Ultimately she was led to Tower Green for execution – but she refused to put her head on the block, declaring: 'So should traitors do, and I am none.' In modern translation she told the axeman to 'catch me if you can' and swivelled her head this way and that to make his job more difficult. It took many blows before her head was severed.

**ONLY WHEN EVIDENCE WAS PRODUCED BY SECRET AGENTS DID A TREASON TRIAL TAKE PLACE. MARY WAS CONVICTED SOME 19 YEARS AFTER ARRIVING IN ENGLAND AND, RELUCTANTLY, ELIZABETH SIGNED THE EXECUTION WARRANT. SHE TOOK NO JOY IN KILLING A SISTER-QUEEN.**

# OF SCOTLAND

for forgiveness she told them: 'I forgive you with all my heart, for now, I hope, you shall make an end of all my troubles.'

With a serene smile, she prepared herself for death. Her ladies-in-waiting removed religious jewellery from her neck and her top clothes until she was stripped to a fulsome petticoat. Mary declared that she had 'never had such grooms to make her unready, and that she never put off her clothes before such a company.' Her loyal attendants could not bear the torment and broke down into tears. Mary soothed them with words spoken in French, embracing each one in turn. Before they withdrew, one pinned a cloth across her face.

Only after the deed was done did the executioner find her small, faithful dog hiding in her petticoats. The hound's hairy coat turned red with blood as it sat between its mistress's head and shoulders, snapping at those trying to retrieve it.

The head was washed and placed on a cushion in one of the windows of the castle for all the crowds to see before being prepared for burial.

**Mary, Queen of Scots, moments before the first of three blows which ended her life.**

# THE SWORD

In Europe the sword was used to administer capital punishment to the upper echelons of society. It was in some ways preferable to the axe. The cut was cleaner because the blade was sharper and therefore death was more immediate.

However, there was no block. Victims of sword executions had to kneel to receive their fate. The faint-hearted who flinched in the final moments of their lives risked a deep and painful gash in the region of their head or shoulders and the ordeal of a second attempt by the executioner. Only the most frail were permitted to sit in a chair.

There were hazards, too, for the assistants of the executioner. If they were called upon to hold down a victim there was considerable risk to their own life or limbs.

## SKILLED SWORDSMAN

In 1501 it was reported that an executioner killed two criminals with a single swing of his mighty sword after positioning them back to back. Unhappily, not all swordsmen possessed the same merciful skills. In France one condemned man volunteered to be an executioner to save his own skin. It took him 29 swings of the sword to execute the Comte de Chalais in 1626.

It was also in France that the Sansons, a celebrated family of executioners, dominated the scaffold. In 1766 Charles-Henri Sanson was confronted by a young man convicted of failing to hail some passing monks on the dubious evidence of a local Lieutenant. The man, Chevalier de la Barre, refused to kneel down, insisting he was no criminal. 'Do your duty,' he told Sanson. 'I shall give you no trouble, only be quick.' Sanson delivered the fatal blow with such skill that the head of the man remained balanced on the shoulders for a few moments before falling to the ground. Witnesses held that Sanson had exclaimed: 'Shake yourself – it's done!'

**VICTIMS HAD TO KNEEL, WITH ONLY THE WEAKEST OFFERED A CHAIR. THE FAINT-HEARTED, WHO FLINCHED AT THE CRUCIAL MOMENT, RISKED PAINFUL GASHES AND THE ORDEAL OF A SECOND ATTEMPT.**

## TOP-HAT KILLERS

German executioners traditionally wore a black frock coat and silk top hat. They were called the Scharfrichter and known as the 'Mate of Death'. The assistant was the Lowe, or lion, who won that name because he would roar when dragging a prisoner in front of a judge. Other duties of the Lowe included rubbish clearance, burying unclaimed bodies and branding criminals.

A typical sword of execution would have had a two inch (5 cm) wide blade which was blunt ended and measured about 40 inches (100 cm) in length. One example from Germany bears an inscription which translates: 'Whenever I raise the sword I wish the sinner everlasting life.'

With the potential for grievous injury so great the era of execution by sword gave way to death by guillotine or by hanging. However, a woman found guilty of poisoning her husband was beheaded by sword in Germany as recently as 1893. Two further murderesses were decapitated with an axe in Germany in 1914.

## MOCK MURDER

**With a coffin in readiness, a French swordsmen delivers a fatal blow to a high-born criminal.**

A reprieve from capital punishment in Germany still brought a savage penalty. The prisoner would undergo the parade to the scaffold, the prayers and even have the headsman wielding a sword above his head in a mock execution.

**133**

# EARLY GUILLOTINES

## THE GUILLOTINE'S COLOURFUL HISTORY BEGAN IN ROMAN TIMES AND A PROTOTYPE OPERATED IN ENGLAND AND SCOTLAND BEFORE ITS DEVELOPMENT IN FRANCE.

Cold metal scything through warm flesh gives a swift and passionless kiss. The guillotine was hailed as a humanitarian milestone when it was introduced in France in 1792. Yet today the vision it conjures of rolling heads and gaping necks makes the blood chill.

The French claimed credit for introducing the guillotine. However, there is evidence that the Romans used a similar device to dispatch one of the apostles, St Matthew. A hefty axe-head was set into grooves running along two upright posts and was propelled downwards after being hit by the executioners' mallet. The same idea of a cross beam and weighted blade was employed by the Persians in the 10th century.

## EARLY IRISH DRAWING

In Ireland in 1307 there was an account made of the execution of one Murcod Ballagh, accompanied by an illustration of a contraption which clearly resembles the famous French guillotine. Indeed, in France itself, there are records showing the use, for execution, of a guillotine-style mechanism as early as 1632. *The Memoires de Puysegur* recount the execution of the Marshal de Montmorenci at Toulouse. 'In that province they make use of a kind of hatchet which runs between two pieces of wood; and when the head is placed on the block below the cord is let go and the hatchet descends and severs the head from the body.'

The most notable forerunner of the guillotine was in use in Halifax, England, from 1286 until 1650. At least 49 people died on the Halifax gibbet (see picture, above) between 20 March 1541 and 30 April 1650, according to parish records.

Above: Even in its crudest forms, the guillotine gave a quick death.

Left: The Halifax Gibbet provides entertainment for on-lookers.

The Halifax gibbet was built around two upright posts five yards (nearly five metres) in length. The blade, which weighed 7 lb 12 oz (3.5 kg) and was 10 inches (25 cm) long, was set on the bottom of a block of wood. When the blade was drawn up it was held in place by a pin attached to a length of rope.

## COLLECTIVE RESPONSIBILITY

Convicted criminals – those who stole goods assessed by four constables to be worth 13½ pence (5½p) or more – were taken to the gibbet on market day for execution. When the offender was placed with his head on the block every man nearby took a hold of the rope and gave a mighty pull to unleash the pin and allow the blade to crash down. If the crime involved the theft of animals then the rope was tied on to the beast in question, or one like it, and the pin removed thus.

## THE SCOTTISH MAIDEN

On seeing the Halifax gibbet in action the Scottish Earl of Morton directed that a similar one should be constructed in Edinburgh. It came into use in 1566 and became known as the Scottish Maiden. Among its first victims were some of the plotters who helped kill Rizzio, favourite secretary of Mary, Queen of Scots.

In total 120 people met their fate by the Maiden, including the Earl of Morton himself. He was accused of complicity in the murder of Darnley, husband of the troubled Scottish Queen, and beheaded in 1581. Another victim was the Earl of Argyll who supported the conspiracy to put James, Duke of Monmouth, on the English throne. Given that it had taken five strokes of the axe to end the life of James, the Earl declared as he knelt to meet his maker that it was the 'sweetest' maiden he had ever kissed.

## HALIFAX HORROR

The Halifax gibbet detached the head from the body with such great force that the head would roll into the crowds, sometimes at speed. A Halifax woman riding along Gibbet Street on a horse suddenly found herself staring at the unseeing eyes of a recently executed man whose head had flown from the block and landed in her saddlebag. More imaginative versions of the story have the woman racked with terror as the corpseless head latches on to her apron with his teeth.

# DR JOSEPH GUILLOTIN

**TODAY HIS NAME CONJURES UP VISIONS OF THE INDISCRIMINATE DEATH WITH WHICH HIS MACHINE IS ASSOCIATED. YET DR JOSEPH GUILLOTIN HOPED HIS INVENTION WOULD EASE THE ANGUISH OF THE CONDEMNED.**

It was with the best of intentions that Dr Joseph Ignace Guillotin pressed for changes in French law regarding the condemned. No longer would there be hanging for the poor, beheading for the rich and the agonies of death on the wheel or at the stake for those convicted of religious crimes.

Instead there would be one punishment for all – decapitation. Dr Guillotin persuaded fellow deputies in the French Constituent Assembly that every person sentenced to death should be beheaded and the ruling became law on 3 May 1791.

**Guillotin was horrified by torturous punishments like the wheel (top) which perpetuated suffering.**

## A HUMANE IDEA

Guillotin was left with the dilemma of how to achieve this genuinely noble sentiment. The sword was no good for multiple executions. It needed to be freshly ground and sharpened each time it was swung. Swinging a sword all day was also physically demanding. And as blood flowed from any initial execution then the subsequent victims would quake and quiver, making it impossible to put them to the sword efficiently. All this information was laid before Guillotin by Charles-Henri Sanson, the Parisian executioner of the day.

Another adviser, Dr Louis from the Academy of Surgery, urged Guillotin to look towards the English models like the Halifax gibbet for his inspiration. 'This apparatus would not be felt and would hardly be perceptible,' Louis declared. Guillotin investigated the method of death across the English Channel, eventually commissioning a German carpenter to build this new and important instrument of death.

Such was the contribution of the good Dr Louis that it was first known as the Louisette. The name Guillotin was soon coined however, shortly to be followed by popular descriptions like 'Red Theatre', 'People's Avenger' and 'National Razor'.

It was certainly similar to the Halifax gibbet in that it had two six inch thick upright posts some ten feet in height and 12 inches apart. The blade was held between each post in runners and was mounted with a 65-lb iron weight to increase its impact. An iron crescent-shaped neck-strap held the victim in position. Here was a state-of-the-art machine, an executioner's dream.

## THE BASCULE

The main refinement on the French model was a bench with a hinged plank called a bascule onto which the victim could be strapped while the plank was upright. Thereafter plank and body were laid down and propelled into the mouth of the guillotine. No matter how faint or fearful, the condemned person was dispatched with minimum fuss. Their British counterparts were compelled to kneel in trepidation.

The blade was held aloft by two ropes each running through brass pulleys. It was when both ropes were released that the guillotine went into action. Sanson was delighted with the prototype and eagerly practised his art on corpses and live animals, including sheep and calves. The guillotine was painted blood-red in preparation for its first victim.

The first of thousands to make the journey of no return to the guillotine was Jacques Pelletier, a highwayman, who was executed on 25 April 1792. Charles-Henri Sanson carried out the grisly deed in the Place de Greve, Paris, already displaying the speed and precision for which he would become famous.

The waiting crowds were less than impressed. The death spectacle was over in a matter of moments and they had seen virtually nothing. As they dispersed they sang: 'Bring me back my wooden gallows.'

**NO FRENCH GUILLOTINE COULD BE COMPLETE WITHOUT A WICKER BASKET BY ITS SIDE IN WHICH TO PLACE THE SEVERED AND BLOODY HEADS OF THE VICTIMS.**

## GUILLOTIN GUILLOTINED?

While Dr Joseph Ignace Guillotin is credited with the creation of the guillotine some believe his cousin, also called Dr Joseph Guillotin, was the prime mover. The second Dr Guillotin was a prison doctor and even travelled to Britain and Scotland to inspect prison regimes where he would have surely encountered the Halifax gibbet and the Scottish Maiden, if only by reputation.

He was a committed revolutionary until he saw the woman he loved beheaded. After that he secretly assisted the Royalists even after the death of the revolution. In 1814 he was tried as a traitor and himself mounted the steps of the guillotine, perhaps victim to his own dread invention?

**FOR TOO LONG THE FRENCH ROYAL FAMILY FRONTED A PROFLIGATE AND DISHONEST REGIME WHICH CONDEMNED THE PEOPLE TO LIVE IN MISERY. FEELINGS RAN HIGH AND ERUPTED INTO REVOLUTION. ALAS FOR THE ARISTOCRACY, THE GUILLOTINE'S INVENTION COINCIDED WITH THE REVOLUTION.**

**Right: France's last king, Louis XVI, attempted reforms but, for the revolutionaries, it was too little, too late.**

**Below, right: Marie Antoinette prays in her cell as she awaits her deadly fate.**

Like many monarchies of the day, the French Royals of the late 18th century were corrupt and inept. Even if King Louis XVI was fair and caring, the government which he endorsed most certainly was not and any attempt at reform was quashed. As the rich grew richer the poor grew bitter and France was ripe for revolution.

The uprising – which began in 1789 with the storming of a state prison called the Bastille – and the overthrow of the King were followed by the most appalling blood-letting. After 1792 executioners were working feverishly to keep up with the death penalties which were meted out by the thousand. The blades of the guillotines were rarely dry.

# VIVE LA

## THE KING'S LAST JOURNEY

First the anger of the mob was directed at members of the royal family and the aristocracy. The King, fearing for his life, tried to flee Paris and reached Varennes but was brought back in shame. He had good reason to seek asylum abroad. On 21 January 1793 his worst fears were realised when he was taken to his death on the guillotine. With him was Henry Essex Edgeworth de Firmont, an Irish-born clergyman requested by the King to offer religious solace.

En route to the guillotine in a carriage fiercely guarded by a body of troops the King devoutly recited psalms. The journey took almost two hours. In the Place de Louis XV the guillotine was waiting, perched high on a scaffold. The eager crowd, armed with primitive weapons like pikes, jostled for position. They were firmly held back by guards who feared a last-minute rescue bid by royalists.

When the King left his carriage three guards approached, intending to disrobe him. They were regally dismissed as the King insisted on taking off his own cloak, untying his necktie and opening his shirt.

The trio loomed again, this time to tie his hands. 'No! I shall never consent to that: do what you have been ordered but you shall never bind me,' the King retorted.

Supported by the clergyman, the King trekked to the scaffold and climbed the steps. Once on top he strode across the platform and silenced the ranks of drummers with a glare.

'I die innocent of all the crimes laid to my charge,' he boldly declared. 'I pardon those who have occasioned my death and I pray to God that the blood you are going to shed may never be visited on France.'

A uniformed official barked an order at the drummers to begin the death roll once more. The last seconds of the King's life were quickly over.

## HATS OFF FOR THE HEAD

A teenage guardsman immediately grabbed the severed head and strutted around the platform with it. Henry Essex described the scene. 'At first an awful silence prevailed; at length some cries of "Vive la Republique!" were heard. By degrees the voices multiplied and in less than ten minutes this cry, a thousand times repeated, became the universal shout of the multitude and every hat was in the air.'

# REPUBLIQUE!

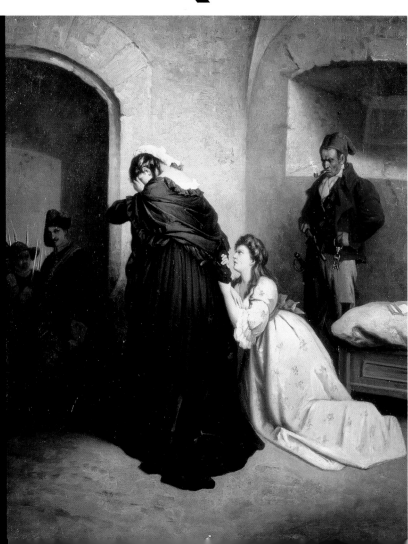

**'LET THEM EAT CAKE' SAID MARIE ANTOINETTE OF THE STARVING PEASANTS. SHE WON NO SYMPATHY FROM THE REBELS WHEN THEY SEIZED CONTROL.**

## MARIE ANTOINETTE

Marie Antoinette, the greedy and lascivious wife of the French king, followed in his footsteps to the guillotine on 16 October 1793. She is most famously remembered for her lack of understanding of the peasant's lot. By the time she journeyed to the guillotine her hair had turned white with worry and her body was emaciated.

# THE REIGN OF ERROR

The blood of the French King did little to appease the revolutionaries. Radicals had seized control of the country. In their pursuit of power they were prepared to sacrifice whoever stood in their way and, after the nobility had been dispatched, they turned their attentions to the citizens. A nation's appetite for blood was whetted and, for a while, appeared to be insatiable.

Most prominent in the murderous regime was Maximilien Robespierre, a lawyer who helped instigate the revolution. Following the death of the King, France was attacked by Prussia and Austria. This hostility prompted the new French rulers to establish a Committee of Public Safety. However this powerful committee became obsessed not with the enemies outside the country's borders but those within.

The Committee brooked no opposition to the revolution. Wave upon wave of French people were produced before courts as neighbour denounced neighbour in an atmosphere heavy with paranoia. More than 50,000 suspects were rounded up in the Reign of Terror and about 2,400 were guillotined in little more than a year.

From the revolutionary tribunals the convicted were taken straight to the guillotine by the cart-load. Astride the coach was the executioner and his assistants. In front was a detachment of horse-guards. To the rear came a coach bearing the Rapporteur and his clerk, charged with witnessing the executions before reporting back to the public accuser, who in Paris was the feared Fouquier-Tinville.

After the cart halted at the foot of the guillotine, the doomed wretches were dealt with one by one. Some needed the help of the executioner's assistants to mount the steps. Many, however, kept their dignity and chose to make the journey unaided. There are reports of smiling, joking victims and some who danced a jig before being strapped to the bascule.

**Maximilien Francois Marie Isidore de Robespierre, leader of the Jacobites, was an engineer of the revolution. After shedding the blood of countless thousands, he was finally denounced in the Legislative Assembly, arrested (above) and died, aged 36, on the guillotine.**

## DEATH OF ROBESPIERRE

The rivers of blood at last sickened sufficient numbers of people to bring about a reversal. Robespierre, who had for a while enjoyed cult-status, was finally reviled as a butcher. He was himself denounced and arrested on 27 July 1794 by an armed contingent. Robespierre was either shot or shot himself during the skirmish and suffered an injury to his jaw. The next day his screams rang out over the Place de la Revolution as Sanson ripped away the dressing to Robespierre's wound. Moments later the tyrant's head was cut off.

## KING OF BEASTS

**THE LAST SYMBOL OF THE MONARCHY IN PARIS WAS A LION FROM THE ROYAL MENAGERIE. HE SURVIVED TO SEE SANITY RETURN TO THE CITY.**

Like a whirlwind, the French Revolution sucked in and spat out all in its path. The aristocracy, the people and later the authors of the bloodshed – both the moderate Girondists and the extreme Jacobins – became victims.

There was, however, one noble survivor. Through weary eyes a lion from the King's menagerie at Versailles witnessed the madness. In 1789, amid anti-Royal fervour, he was moved to Paris and put on public view.

As the 'king of beasts' and one of the last living vestiges of the French royal family he was reviled, poked and insulted throughout the revolution. By the end he was suffering from mange and was almost paralysed by painful sores and blisters.

But for him and the rest of the French people who endured the revolution there was hope. And by 1800 he was enjoying a new home at a zoological park where he was well looked after.

# SANSON AND SON

The executioner's job in France was very much a family affair. Fathers passed on their skills to their sons who married daughters from other executioners' families. Six generations of the Sanson family held the post in Paris between 1688 and 1889. At the time of the revolution the incumbent was Charles-Henri Sanson.

Charles-Henri, who succeeded his father Jean Baptiste in 1778, was both well educated and musically inclined. Fashionably dressed, he could afford to live well enough on his salary of 10,000 livres a year although he was poorer than his father had been after an executioner's tax on foodstuffs was abolished in 1775. He was courted by leading lights of society, despite his grisly trade – he was not only master of the guillotine but also the public torturer too.

However, his contribution to the revolution was not enthusiastically made. Throughout his career Charles-Henri, known as 'Monsieur de Paris' or 'Charlot', remained sensitive to the suffering of those he was about to dispatch and was particularly distressed to see women beheaded.

# PROFESSIONAL PRIDE

Although he was sickened by the scale of bloodshed, Sanson was determined to carry out his work professionally.

When the leading Girondist, Georges Danton, tried to embrace condemned colleague Marie-Jean Herault de Sechelles upon the scaffold the pair were pulled apart by Sanson. The courts were the place for political posturing, Sanson believed, not the foot of the guillotine. Wryly, Danton remarked to his friend: 'They will not prevent our heads from meeting in the basket'.

Apparently undaunted by the fate that awaited him Danton, with his shirt marked by the blood of his closest allies, told Sanson: 'Don't forget to show my head to the people. It is well worth the trouble.'

**Left: Reluctantly, Sanson was at his post during the execution of the King.**

**Above: The executioner pulls the pin to release the blade. It was also his job to show the crowd the victim's head.**

## QUICK WORK

Sanson could not help but be satisfied with the performance of the guillotine. One day he cut off 22 heads in just 36 minutes, a tribute to its efficiency.

# RIVERS OF BLOOD

The executioner's working conditions were all but impossible during the Reign of Terror. Blood soaked the scaffold, leaving Sanson and his assistants liable to slip and fall. Indeed, in 1792 Charles-Henri saw his own son Gabriel tumble to the ground, sustaining fatal injuries, after skidding in a pool of blood. Afterwards, railings were put up around scaffolds to safeguard executioners.

Blood gathered in a pond beneath the scaffold, causing a disgusting stench. Rivers of it ran down the cobbled streets. At the peak of the Terror Sanson guillotined 300 men and women in three days. Had he objected, Sanson knew full well that his own head would be on the block.

It was Sanson who executed the King, a task he did not relish. He retired three years later in favour of his son Henri. The job then passed to Henri's son Clement-Henri who, short of cash, pawned his guillotine. When he was unable to carry out his civic duty he was fired in disgrace. The Sanson dynasty was at an end, although the guillotine lived on.

# THE SPECTACLE AT THE GUILLOTINE

The guillotine was exported to other countries, among them Italy. Author Charles Dickens witnessed an execution in Rome on 8 March 1845. In his description of the event he told how he reached the appointed spot at 7.30 am in good time for the execution, scheduled for 8.45 am. The accused man had apparently confessed under the inquisition of Papal monks to robbing and killing a countess.

The guillotine was erected in a back street within sight of a church. Dickens was struck at the sight of it. 'An untidy, unpainted, uncouth, crazy-looking thing of course, some seven feet high, perhaps, with a tall, gallows-shaped frame rising above it in which was the knife, charged with a ponderous mass of iron, all ready to descend and glittering brightly in the morning sun, whenever it looked out, now and then, from behind a cloud.'

A small crowd gathered as the time ticked by. A cigar seller and a baker plied their wares. When 11 am struck on the church clock it seemed the execution might have been cancelled or postponed. Yet suddenly marching soldiers arrived and lined the scaffold.

The prisoner followed behind in a procession of monks who held a crucifix aloft. His shirt had been cut away, his hands were tied and his feet bare. Without delay he knelt down so his neck could be secured in the device. A few seconds later he was beheaded. Grasping the head by the hair, the executioner paraded around the scaffold before putting it on a pole. A bloody mess left behind was washed down with buckets of water by one of the attendants.

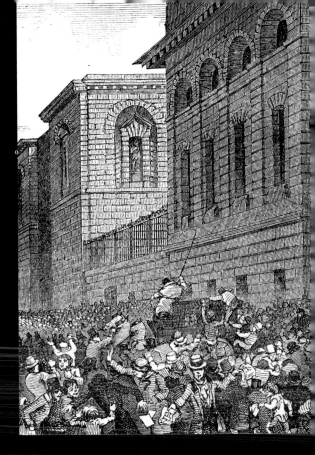

For a while at least it seemed the baying hoards would never tire of seeing blood spilled. All over Europe the spectacle of a guillotining or public execution drew vast numbers. It would be years before state-sponsored killings were carried out behind closed doors.

'IT IS A FAR FAR BETTER THING THAT I DO THAN I HAVE EVER DONE. IT IS A FAR FAR BETTER REST THAT I GO TO THAN I HAVE EVER KNOWN.'

– SYDNEY CARTON AT THE GUILLOTINE IN DICKENS' *TALE OF TWO CITIES*.

## DISGUST OF DICKENS

'Nobody cared or was at all affected,' wrote Dickens. 'There was no manifestation of disgust, or pity, or indignation, or sorrow.'

Dickens grew to loath public executions and was particularly appalled at the unruly behaviour of the crowds. After Frederick and Maria Manning were hanged for murder at Horsemonger Lane, Dickens wrote to *The Times* expressing his disgust.

'The horrors of the gibbet and of the crime which brought the wretched murderers to it faded in my mind before the atrocious bearing, looks and language of the assembled spectators…

'When the day dawned thieves, low prostitutes, ruffians and vagabonds of every kind flock on the ground, with every variety of offensive and foul behaviour…When the sun rose brightly it gilded thousands upon thousands of upturned faces, so inexpressibly odious in their brutal mirth or callousness that a man had cause to feel ashamed of the shape he wore.'

## INSTANT DEATH?

Death by guillotine was fast. But the question of just how fast perplexed doctors for decades. Could the victims function after their heads were severed from their shoulders?

One 19th century opponent of the guillotine declared that: 'Death is not instantaneous…every vital element survives decapitation…It is a savage vivisection followed by premature burial'.

There are numerous tales about lips moving, eyes blinking and a variety of twitching from corpses after the impact of the guillotine or axe. French doctors were keen to establish that the brain was still working by way of a delayed reaction. They tried to verify their theories with some primitive 'scientific' experiments. At executions they secured a ringside seat in order to call out the name of the victim immediately after the blade had fallen. Some reported that the eyes opened and focused for thirty seconds or more after decapitation. Other medics ghoulishly pumped blood into a recently severed head in order to monitor its reactions.

Three doctors made a study of the issue after an execution and reported in the *British Medical Journal* in December 1879: 'We have ascertained, as far as is humanely possible to do so, that the head of the criminal in question had no semblance whatever of the sense of feeling; that the eyes lost the power of vision; and, in fact, the head was perfectly dead to all intents and purposes.' It was without doubt a mercifully quicker process than hanging.

**FRENCH DOCTORS WERE KEEN TO ESTABLISH THAT THE BRAIN WAS STILL WORKING BY WAY OF DELAYED REACTION.**

# THE GUILLOTINE AT VERSAILLES

By law French executions were held publicly. And even during the 20th century guillotining has attracted enormous milling crowds.

There were rituals adopted by the French government which specified that the place of execution should be outside the condemned man's prison, the hour early in the morning to avoid a clamour in the crowd and the news of its impending occurrence kept from the prisoner himself.

These procedures were adopted when Landru, the notorious 'Bluebeard', was executed on 25 February 1922. When word that the final appeal for clemency had been turned down late on 24 February, journalists and spectators set off for Versailles where dark streets were already thronging with people, just like a market day. It was there that Landru was held in jail.

At 4 am Anatole Deibler, the goat-bearded executioner who had dispatched more than 300 criminals during his time, arrived at the jail. Deibler lived in Versailles under an assumed name and kept the tool of his trade in his garden shed. And still Landru knew nothing of his impending fate.

**Henri Landru, known as 'Bluebeard', died less than half a minute from being whisked from the prison gates to the guillotine.**

## TICKET-ONLY VIEWING

Workmen bolted together the struts of the guillotine by lamplight. Although they worked hurriedly it took an hour to complete the task. Deibler, in his characteristic white gloves, hauled on the ropes to position the blade. A select ticket-only crowd gathered at the foot of the guillotine, with its posts 12 feet (four metres) high. The rest were kept back by infantry and horseguards with sabres drawn.

At 5.45 am a deputation arrived at the door of Landru's cell. Although no warning had been delivered, Landru sat up and said: 'I know, gentlemen, why you have come. There is no need to tell me. I am an innocent man but I will die bravely. I know that this is not your fault and I forgive you.'

Landru asked to be shaved. Brushing aside the customary cigarette and rum offered to those about to die, Landru spent a few moments alone with a chaplain before being led to his fate. Wearing a shirt with its neck cut away and a pair of cheap, dark trousers, Landru walked barefoot to the guillotine with his arms tied behind his back.

His lawyer lent forward and whispered: 'Courage'. Landru replied: 'Thanks, Maitre, I have always had that.'

Moments before the prison gates swung open, the guillotine was given a test run. Then Landru appeared, his face waxy, flanked by two prison guards. They walked with him, as fast as they were able, to the guillotine where he was bundled against the plank and swung into position.

With a fearful clunk and thud, the execution was completed. Both parts of the body were hastily put in a horse-drawn van and were driven away at a gallop. One observer timed the proceedings. Landru died just 26 seconds after he had first appeared in the prison courtyard.

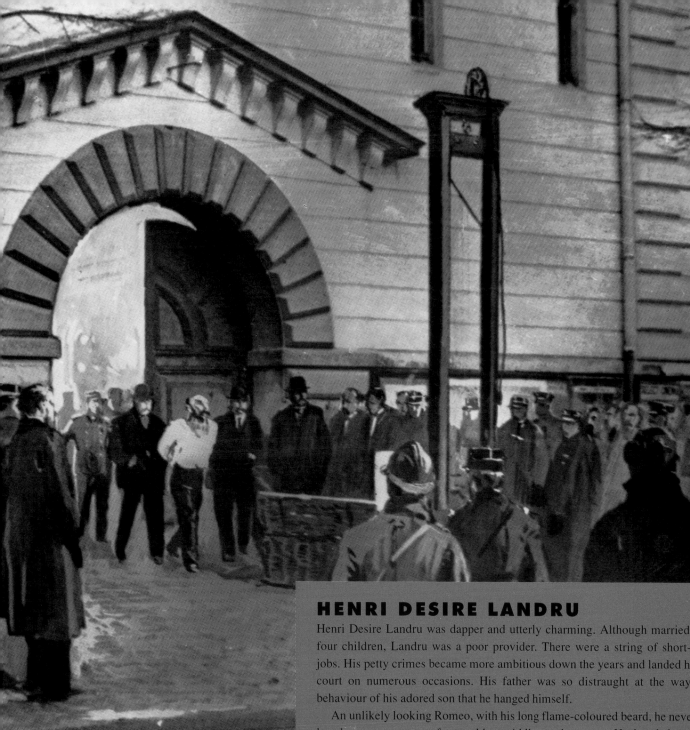

**POLICE FOUND 290 FRAGMENTS OF BONES AND TEETH IN THE STOVE AS WELL AS CLOTHES AND PERSONAL POSSESSIONS AROUND THE HOUSE.**

## HENRI DESIRE LANDRU

Henri Desire Landru was dapper and utterly charming. Although married with four children, Landru was a poor provider. There were a string of short-lived jobs. His petty crimes became more ambitious down the years and landed him in court on numerous occasions. His father was so distraught at the wayward behaviour of his adored son that he hanged himself.

An unlikely looking Romeo, with his long flame-coloured beard, he nevertheless became a magnet for wealthy, middle-aged women. He lured them with advertisements in 'lonely hearts' columns. 'Widower, with two children, aged forty-three, possessing comfortable income, affectionate, serious and moving in good society, desires to meet widow of similar status, with a view to matrimony.'

Widow Jeanne Cuchet answered the published plea. She was bowled over. But when all her wealth and goods were signed over to him, Landru killed her and her 17-year-old son Andre at Vernouillet, burning their bodies on the house fire. In that same year, 1915, there were two other murders. Landru then moved to the Villa Ermitage at Gambais where a further seven women were dispatched.

Landru was captured on 12 April 1919 after the mayor of Gambais began to probe the mystery resident and his numerous lady friends. Police found 290 fragments of bones and teeth in the stove as well as clothes and personal possessions around the house. A question mark remains on the exact number of his victims.

His trial took place at the Seine-et-Oise Assize Court in November 1921. During lengthy interrogations by police he never admitted his guilt. Nevertheless, he was found guilty and sentenced to death.

From his cell Landru penned a drawing and presented it to his defence counsel. In 1963 the daughter of the attorney had the picture cleaned and there, on the back, appeared a line of confession written in Landru's own hand.

## A GORY DISPLAY OF LIFE-LIKE SEVERED HEADS WAS A CROWD-PULLER IN THE 1790S. THE CHAMBER OF HORRORS HOLDS THE SAME APPEAL TODAY.

'One man's dead is another man's bread'. So the saying goes in Europe and it is never more true than when talking about the guillotine.

The guillotine quickly became a symbol of high fashion. Scale models were made to cut cigars. Dr Joseph Ignace Guillotin was delighted to illustrate the finer points of his brain child at society dinner parties up and down Paris using just such a device.

Miniature replicas were sold on street corners as children's toys – complete with live sparrows on which to practise. Women sought to have working models on their mantelpieces. The son of doomed queen Marie Antoinette is known to have played with a little guillotine only months before his mother met her death on the real thing.

It was entirely due to the over-exertions of the executioners during the revolutionary years that the waxworks museum created by Madame Tussaud won fame and fortune. Madame Tussaud was born Marie Grosholtz in Switzerland. Her mother was housekeeper to Dr Philippe Curtius who moved from Berne, Switzerland, to Paris some 10 years before the revolution to start a waxworks exhibition.

As Marie grew up she displayed a talent for modelling which captivated Dr Curtius, whom she called 'Uncle'. Her skills were put to good use in the Salon de Cire – her 'Uncle's' exhibition – which featured famous folk of the day. That was until she was employed at Versailles by the French princess Elizabeth as a tutor in art. Only when the revolution began and she was released from Royal duties was she able to assist her 'Uncle' once more.

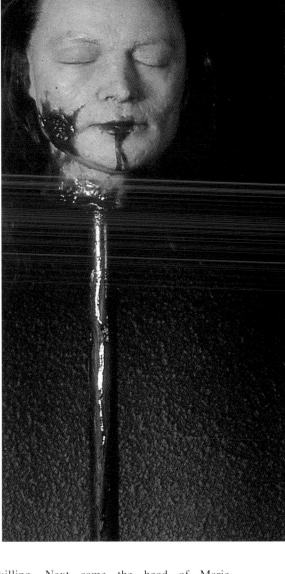

## CRIMINAL DEATH MASKS

In 1783 Curtius opened a *Caverne des Grands Voleurs*, displaying effigies of notorious criminals of the day. Executioner Charles-Henri Sanson gave Curtius access to the bodies of dead criminals for financial reward. This new exhibition was an instant hit. When revolutionary violence erupted in 1789 young Marie was presented with the severed heads of hated royalists by the mob to make death masks.

After 1792 her inspiration became the victims of the guillotine. She worked with Curtius to take a plaster death mask of King Louis XVI, on the orders of the ruling National Assembly.

Marie's small hands went to work when the revolutionary Marat was stabbed in his bath. She also took a mask of Charlotte Corday, the woman who was sent to the guillotine for the

killing. Next came the head of Marie Antoinette and later, that of Hebert, a revolutionary who found his way to the guillotine because he opposed Robespierre. Each was transformed into a lifelike wax model.

In 1794 Marie and her mother were suddenly arrested. Curtius, a committed revolutionary, was on a government mission out of Paris and was unable to intervene. It was the fall from grace of Robespierre that saved them from the scaffold. Marie was released in time to take his death mask which won pride of place in the waxworks museum.

That same year her mentor, Curtius, died and left everything to Marie. She continued to take death masks of the notorious victims of the guillotine. The list included Fouquier-Tinville, the feared public prosecutor.

**Entrepreneur Dr Philippe Curtius tutored Madame Tussaud in the art of death masks.**

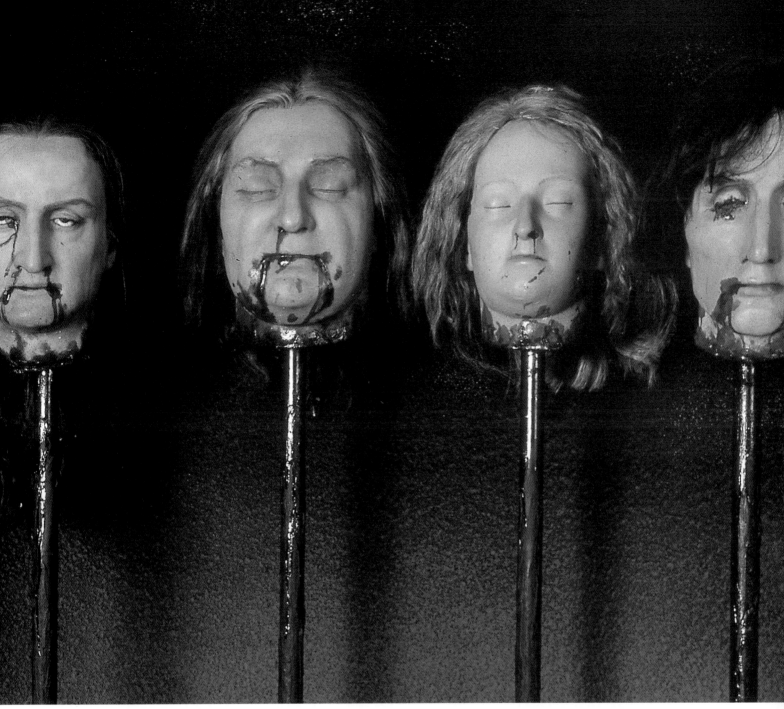

## MADAME TUSSAUD'S IN LONDON

Marie married Francois Tussaud in 1795. Her husband did little to support her, her mother and their two sons, so Marie took the waxworks exhibition to London. She was to tour through England, Scotland and Ireland for much of the remainder of her life – and she continued to take death masks of notorious British criminals including the celebrated Cato Street conspirator Arthur Thistlewood and the body snatcher William Hare. Before she died in 1850 aged 89 years, Madame Tussaud had heard her waxworks hall of infamy coined in *Punch* magazine as 'The Chamber of Horrors'. Among the most popular exhibits were the victims of the guillotine in revolutionary France (above).

# HANGING

It started with nothing more than a tree and a length of rope. Today hanging is a scientific art, developed over the centuries into a quick, clean mode of death.

Early man meted out vengeance on his neighbour by hanging – he simply threaded a rope across a branch and hoisted his victim, with a noose around the neck, off the ground. Death usually came about through strangulation. This kind of primitive 'justice' was still used by lynch mobs many centuries later.

The first signs of a scientific approach came during Anglo-Saxon times when a ladder was used in tandem with a purpose-built wooden gallows. Now the condemned man was forced up the ladder which was subsequently 'turned out' so he lost his footing and fell to his death.

However, the fall was a short one. In some cases the victim's neck was broken but this was rare. As before, death – which was slow and painful – was usually due to strangulation.

## THE TRIPLE TREE AT TYBURN

The ladder was a feature of death by hanging for years to come. It was used in conjunction with the first triangular shaped scaffolds which emerged in the latter half of the 16th century. Elaborating on the same design, the Triple Tree at Tyburn – with its three cross beams each measuring nine feet (three metres) and having space for up to 24 victims – appeared soon afterwards.

In the 17th century a cart replaced the ladder and the entire process was speeded up. Prisoners were transported to the gallows by horse-driven cart and remained on it while the hangman's assistant perched atop the cross beam to secure the loose end of the rope. Once that had been done, the executioner whipped the back of the horses and they moved away at a gallop, leaving the victims dangling by their necks in the air. To hasten death and reduce suffering, the executioner and his assistant would sometimes pull down the legs of the doomed wretches. Mostly they were left to suffer until death prevailed.

There were those left troubled by the evident anguish suffered by men and women enduring a slow death on the gallows. Matters improved when a doctor decreed the knot of the noose should be placed to the right or left side of the neck, below the ear, in order to quicken the process. During the 18th century it became the rule rather than the exception for the victim to have his or her face covered by a white cap before the hanging.

**TO HASTEN DEATH, THE EXECUTIONER AND HIS ASSISTANT WOULD SOMETIMES PULL DOWN THE LEGS OF THE DOOMED WRETCHES.**

**Left: Already in his shroud, condemned man Stephen Gardiner makes a final speech at Tyburn before the cart is driven from beneath him.**

## THE BLACK ACTS

In Britain in the 18th century, the number of capital offences on the statute book rose to its highest level as Parliament sought to protect property. Anyone guilty of attempted murder might well be looked upon leniently by the courts while a man guilty of forgery, poaching, burning down a hayrick or even cutting down an ornamental shrub would be condemned to death. The crimes deemed punishable by death were greatly increased by the Waltham Black Act of 1723. For good measure, the act said that anyone who appeared on the highway with a sooty face could be put to death. It was the excesses of this Act that helped reduce the number of capital deaths as juries, judges and even victims sought to reduce the charges against villains or find them 'not guilty' rather than see them hang for a trifling offence.

## FINAL STYLE

Those who went boldly to the gallows won the hearts and minds of the mob. An Italian count was impressed with the fortitude shown by the majority that were hanged. Of their appearance he wrote: '(They are) as if going to be married, with the calmest indifference in the world.'

# THE SCIENCE OF HANGING

**Earl Ferrers (above right) died slowly because the short drop left his toes touching the ground. The system was improved by the time this pirate (above) met his death.**

A major innovation in the history of hanging was the drop, first appearing in 1760 at the execution of the 4th Earl Ferrers. There was a raised section on the platform of the gallows which opened, leaving the victim suspended.

The inaugural hanging was marred by two things. Firstly, an unseemly squabble between executioner Thomas Turlis and his assistant over a five guinea tip from the Earl. Next, the length of the drop proved too short. After the platform fell away the unfortunate Earl could still touch the ground with his toes. Turlis and his assistant wasted no time in pulling down

on the legs of the Earl. Still, one bystander thought it took at least four minutes for the nobleman-turned-killer to die.

Turlis returned to the old-style cart method of dispatch. But when gallows were built outside Newgate jail in 1783 they were of the short drop design. In those days the executioner would disappear below the platform to release the bolt on the drop door. He might then appear clutching at the body of the hanged man. Much later the more efficient double flaps were introduced and, later still, the railway-style handle flap release.

## CALCULATING THE DROP

Across the Irish sea there were experiments with the 'long' drop. Death was instantaneous but sometimes the fall was so violent that the head was severed. Cobbler-turned-executioner Thomas Marwood, who hanged his first victim at Lincoln in 1871, imported the idea of the long drop to England. He cared sufficiently about those he dispatched to wish them a swift death. He found that a drop of about eight feet was generally the most successful in achieving this.

With care, he calculated the precise length of rope needed, taking into account the weight and height of the felon and the muscular strength of the neck. He also discovered that a metal ring, carefully positioned on the noose, was a faster, more efficient route to death than the traditional hangman's knot.

Decades later trainee executioners were taught the science of hanging. A ready reckoner table helped them work out the length of hemp rope needed for a successful execution. A chalk mark indicating the exact centre of the trap doors, directly in line with the rope, ensured the body did not swing but plunged directly downwards. Including the time it took to apply arm and leg restraints, a condemned man could enter the execution room and meet his maker in as little as eight seconds.

## LONDON'S CONDEMNED

Between 1749 and 1758 almost 70 per cent of those sentenced to death in London and Middlesex died dangling on the end of a rope – some 365 people. Fifty years on there were no fewer than 804 capital convictions, reflecting the huge rise in the city's population. Yet only 126 were hanged, just 15 per cent.

**THERE WERE EXPERIMENTS WITH THE 'LONG' DROP. DEATH WAS INSTANTANEOUS BUT SOMETIMES THE HEAD WAS SEVERED.**

## EXECUTIONER'S VIEW

'I operated, on behalf of the State, what I am convinced was the most humane and the most dignified method of meting out death to a delinquent – however justified or unjustified the allotment of death may be – and on behalf of humanity I trained other nations to adopt the British system of execution…The fruit of my experience has this bitter after-taste; that I do not now believe that any one of the hundreds of executions I carried out has in any way acted as a deterrent against future murder. Capital punishment, in my view, achieved nothing except revenge.'

– Albert Pierrepoint, the British hangman until his resignation in 1956, in his biography *Executioner Pierrepoint*.

# THE HANGMAN

Whether they be John, Tom or William, executioners in Britain have for years been known by the name Jack or, to be precise, Jack Ketch. The original Jack Ketch was a bungling executioner who took office in London in the autumn of 1663. He had delusions of grandeur, adopting the title 'Esquire' and describing himself on occasion as 'Sir' Ketch. His skills with the axe were woefully lacking as Lord William Russell and the Duke of Monmouth discovered.

Axes were crudely made and bore a cutting edge that was far from sharp. Rather than slicing, it smashed through the neck. Without a degree of skill from the executioner it could be an agonising death. Ketch never mastered the art so he always inflicted a deeply painful departure, butchering and botching.

When it came to the execution of Monmouth, Ketch struck three blows without killing his victim, then flung down the axe claiming he could not do it. Only threats from the outraged officials compelled him to continue. Five blows were struck in the end before Ketch resorted to a knife to sever the head completely.

And he cared little for the sufferings of his victims. It was his lot to execute the 35 innocent dignitaries falsely accused by the anti-Catholic Titus Oates of treason against King Charles II in the Popish plot.

**HE HAD DELUSIONS OF GRANDEUR, ADOPTING THE TITLE 'ESQUIRE'. HIS SKILLS WITH THE AXE WERE WOEFULLY LACKING, HOWEVER, AS HIS VICTIMS DISCOVERED. AND KETCH WAS NOT ABOVE THE LAW AS HE WAS ARRESTED (LEFT) FOR DRUNKENESS.**

**William Marwood, a humane hangman, developed the 'long drop' which led to a speedy death by a snapped neck rather than the pain of strangulation.**

## EARLIER EXECUTIONERS

Many of the early executioners were themselves crooks. Cratwell, one of the busy executioners of King Henry VIII, who was in the post about a century before Ketch, was himself hung for robbery after four years spent in the job.

In 1611 Gregory Brandon became executioner in London. Brandon believed he was of Royal stock, with his father being the illegitimate son of the Duke of Suffolk, a brother-in-law to King Henry VIII. It was 'Old Gregory' who delivered the death blow to Sir Walter Raleigh. On his death in 1640 the post went to his son Richard, otherwise known as 'Young Gregory'. As a child Richard craved to be an executioner and polished up his skills practising on cats and dogs.

A father and his two sons were tried in Derby for horse-stealing. A sadistic judge offered to pardon the one who would hang the other two. The father refused, appalled at the thought of taking away the life he had given. The elder son too turned down his chance of freedom, hating the notion of killing his father. Yet the younger son, John Crosland, seized his opportunity and carried out the court's ruling. He became one of the most hated and heartless men of the city until his death in 1705.

## LADY BETTY

In Connaught, Ireland, a woman presided over the hangings. 'Lady Betty' had originally been brought to justice after killing a lodger at her home for his savings. The dead fellow turned out to be her own son, whom she had treated so harshly in boyhood that he had enlisted in the army. On his return he remained incognito to discover whether or not his mother had softened over the years. He learned to his cost that she had not.

She was to be executed with others. But when the day dawned, no executioner could be found. Betty volunteered and saved her skin. Thereafter she carried out all the hangings, floggings and other punishments in the area.

# HANGMAN'S GALLERY

After Ketch had done his worst, the condemned in London were served by John Hooper who was nicknamed 'Jolly Jack'. He always had a grin or a joke as he stood on the scaffold, not to belittle his victims but to lighten their load.

Then there was John Price, the hangman and *bon viveur* who ran up debts and finally turned to robbery. He was himself hanged on 3 May 1718, a shining example that the deterrent effect of capital punishment is over-estimated.

Thomas Turlis, London's executioner from 1752, first used the platform drop. His successor was Edward Dennis, a man with a lucky star. Dennis, caught up in the anti-Catholic riots of 1780, turned looter and was hauled before the courts. The sentence was hanging, as Dennis knew it must be. From his isolation cell in jail he begged that his son might take the job of hangman. But the authorities deemed it inappropriate that a son should be asked to hang his own father.

JAMES BOTTING WAS ONE OF THE BLACKEST MEN TO STROLL ON THE SCAFFOLD, REVELLING IN HIS ROLE AS DELIVERER OF DEATH. WHEN HE· RETIRED HE WAS SHUNNED BY ALL.

That decision was to be the salvation of Dennis. For, when there was no one to carry out the orders of the court regarding himself and the other rioters, Dennis was released to continue his work.

This was not uncommon. Ned Barlow, the reviled hangman of Lancaster, stood before the courts in March 1806 charged with stealing a horse. He was found guilty and sentenced to death. But who could carry out the sentence? The penalty was changed to a 10-year prison term during which Ned was allowed leave from jail to carry on hanging.

Following Dennis was William Brunskill, a former assistant hangman who nevertheless was somewhat short on skill. It took Governor Wall 15 minutes to die after the noose knot slipped behind his neck in an execution at which Brunskill officiated. He also hanged Colonel Despard, a famous traitor, and John Bellingham, the assassin of Britain's Prime Minister Spencer Perceval.

In 1814 John Langley became executioner after Brunskill died. He is perhaps best remembered for appointing James Botting as assistant. For Botting, as assistant and later as executioner, was one of the blackest men to stroll on the scaffold. He clearly revelled in his work. Even after he retired he was shunned by the criminal fraternity, colleagues and neighbours. His bloody tenure ended when he got into debt.

**Calcraft was a bootmender by trade who turned 'executioner to Her Majesty'.**

## TIME LINE – HANGING IN BRITAIN

**1571** Triple tree at Tyburn first used

**1752** Murder Act – permitting bodies to go for dissection by surgeons

**1759** Triple tree pulled down

**1780** Last execution at Tower Hill

**1868** Public hangings abolished

**1964** Last person to be hanged in Britain

**1969** Capital punishment abolished

**BERRY WAS A DEVOUT CHRISTIAN AND BECAME CONVINCED THAT HE HAD HANGED INNOCENT MEN. HE LONGED TO SEE THE END OF CAPITAL PUNISHMENT.**

## LONG SERVICE – SHORT ROPE

His assistant Foxen took over the job after Botting landed up in a debtor's prison. After Foxen came William Calcraft who held the executioner's job for a mammoth 45 years from 1829. Calcraft's first victim on the gallows was wearing a straight-jacket. Esther Hibber had been so violent since being arrested for the murder of a workhouse child that all around her were in peril. When Calcraft did his duty the crowd rang with chants of 'Good old Calcraft' and he was given three cheers!

Calcraft it was who carried out the last public hanging in 1868, that of Michael Barrett in front of Newgate jail. He used such short lengths of rope that his victims were always painfully strangled. Wearing flamboyant clothes and with a joke or an obscenity on his lips, Calcraft became an unpopular figure.

Dickens was moved to state: 'Mr Calcraft should be restrained in his unseemly briskness, in his jokes, his oaths and his brandy.'

Marwood was Calcraft's successor, the pioneer of the long drop. His friend James Berry took over the post in 1884, to hang 200 prisoners during the eight years he was in office. Berry was deeply religious and became convinced that he had hanged innocent men. After he resigned in 1892 he became a lay preacher and was fervently against capital punishment. He died in 1913 longing to see its abolition in Britain.

**Calcraft spent 45 years in the executioner's post but earned a reputation for cracking sick jokes and drinking too much.**

# THE EXECUTIONER'S LOT

Executioners were both heroes and villains. Those who carried out the death penalty on despicable crooks earned the support of the mob which turned up to watch. But if the criminal were a popular fellow then it was hangman, beware, for the unruly crowd might instantly seek to avenge a death.

It was not uncommon for hangmen to wear masks, false beards or other disguises to protect their identity. The dilemma of the executioner was increased when, in Britain after 1752, the bodies of murderers were destined by law to go under the surgeon's knife. Enraged family and friends of the victims were likely to pounce as the executioner cut them down to hand the bodies over to the surgeon's go-between.

On occasion the executioner was even in danger from the person he was hanging. Hannah Dagoe, sentenced to death for robbery, had attacked warders and fellow convicts in jail and turned the full force of her well-built frame on Thomas Turlis as the cart stopped beneath the gallows. It was several frenzied minutes before he could restrain her.

## THE PERKS OF THE JOB

Executioners were also responsible for carrying out other punishments, including flogging. The pay and privileges of the executioner left him financially secure. Apart from the money he was paid, there were many perks, although these were slowly eroded down the years. The hangman was entitled to have the clothing of the condemned and any other property they had on them at the time. If the victim were notorious, these could be sold as souvenirs, along with the rope.

Usually a house came with the job and he was allowed to claim a tax from local tradesmen which would keep him in food and fuel. Before the 1752 'Murder Act' illicit deals

with surgeons not only disposed of the corpses but helped to line the hangman's pocket.

Wealthier clients happily tipped their hangman. Some local councils even paid a pension! More than 200 offences carried the death penalty in Britain by the end of the 18th century – even the lowly offence of writing on Westminster bridge was a capital crime – so hangmen and headsmen up and down the country had ample work.

The executioners would argue that they had expenses to meet; the cost of assistants, ropes, transport and so forth. He might save some cash with workaday criminals and re-use the rope. It became mandatory to use a new rope

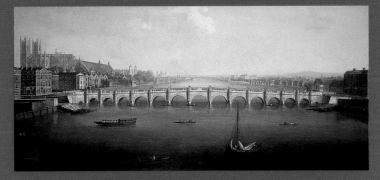

for each hanging only in 1890. But there was always the chance of a reprieve for the condemned man which would have the executioner jobless for a day.

At the start of the 18th century the post was worth about £40 a year. William Calcraft was paid a guinea a week by the City of London plus a guinea for each execution he carried out. Floggings were worth a half-a-crown to him. His reputation took him to other parts of the country, too, and each execution out of London earned him a fat fee.

Marwood earned £10 for each execution – though the number of executions was fast declining as the felonies warranting the death penalty decreased – as well as enjoying a retaining fee.

**Left: Among the tasks of the executioner was flogging and branding. At a time when drawing grafitti on Westminster Bridge (above) was a capital offence, there was plenty of work to do.**

# CONTEMPORARY TERMS AND SLANG

## Executioner
Jack Ketch, Finisher of the Law, Surveyor of the New Drop, Yeoman of the Halter, Topping Fellow, Scragboy, Doomster, Dempster, Lord of the Scaffold.

## Execution day
A Hanging Match, Collar Day, Sheriff's Ball, Hanging Fair, Paddington Fair (Tyburn being in the parish of Paddington), Scrag'em Fair.

## Gallows
Gregorian Tree, Deadly Never-green.

## To hang
To swing, to dance the Paddington frisk, to dance upon nothing, to go up the ladder to rest, to Morris, to dance the Newgate hornpipe, to go west, to ride a horse foaled by an acorn, to dangle in the Sheriff's picture frame, to cry cockles, to be jammed, to be frummagemmed, to be collared, to be noozed, to be scragged, to be stretched, to be ucked up, to be turned off, to die of hempen fever, to take the earth bath, to shake a cloth in the wind.

## Hanged men
Gallows apples, Jack Ketch's pippins.

# THE CONDEMNED

As a condemned man lay in squalor at Newgate jail the night before his execution, the midnight black was punctured by doleful chimes. It was the bellman from nearby St Sepulchre's Church (below) who was sounding his handbell and reading aloud these woeful words.

*All you that in the condemned hold do lie*
*Prepare you, for tomorrow you shall die.*
*Watch all, and pray, the hour is drawing near*
*That you before th'Almighty must appear.*
*Examine well yourselves, in time repent,*
*That you may not t'eternal flames be sent;*
*And when St Sepulchre's bell tomorrow tolls,*
*The Lord have mercy on your souls!*

It was all part of the service provided by St Sepulchre's thanks to one Robert Dove, a Merchant Taylor of London. In 1604 he gave £50 to the parish to ensure that this verse was read three times to the condemned before they set off for Tyburn, in the hope that they might seek redemption.

Those due to die were also likely to have attended the Condemned Sermon in the chapel of Newgate on the Sunday prior to the execution – when part of the burial service was usually read. As if they needed reminding of their grim fate, prisoners sat in a pew painted black. They were of great interest to the rest of the congregation. When notorious villains were in the pew, attendance at the chapel was by ticket only.

Even at this late stage there was hope for a reprieve. During the 18th century it was so common for death sentences to be commuted to a jail term or transportation that only around one in seven condemned men reached Tyburn.

**IN 1830 SIR ROBERT PEEL (LEFT) STATED: 'IT IS IMPOSSIBLE TO CONCEAL FROM OURSELVES THAT CAPITAL PUNISHMENTS ARE MORE FREQUENT AND THE CRIMINAL LAW MORE SEVERE ON THE WHOLE IN THIS COUNTRY THAN IN ANY COUNTRY IN THE WORLD.'**

## THE TRIP TO TYBURN

On execution days, as the procession left for Tyburn, the great bell of St Sepulchre's Church tolled a dozen times, a practice which marked executions until 1890. In the early days, prisoners were dragged to Tyburn behind a horse. But when there were too many fatalities – and much disgust voiced in the disappointed crowds who felt deprived of a show – a cart was introduced. There were stopping points for drinks, including the hospital of St Giles in the Fields. This was a tradition begun by Matilda, wife of Henry I, who decreed that a 'cup of charity' should be offered to the condemned.

The convict sat in the cart, often perched on his coffin, with his arms tied, facing the back. That way he was spared the sight of the scaffold looming ever larger and the authorities were spared escape attempts by terror-struck prisoners. Uttering words of comfort was a clergyman at his side. Around his waist was bound the rope by which he would hang. At the head of the procession rode the city marshal or sheriff and his deputy in the company of the hangman, followed by a troop of staff-bearing constables. At the rear were more armed constables.

## THE LAST DANCE

Hauled on to the gallows with the baying crowd arrayed before him, even the stoutest heart must have quailed. Yet there are accounts of men who have danced and joked to please the hordes. There was time for last speeches. Many convicts began rambling monologues in the hope that a last-minute reprieve would be granted. It was known that the authorities would delay granting reprieves until the last possible moment, to make the punishment more acute. A long farewell was never popular with the crowd, however, and most were numbed into silence.

A white hood was drawn over their faces so their lolling tongues and pinched expressions during the death throes were hidden from the mob. It was time to die.

**Sightings of angels and blazing lights were reported by those who survived the gallows.**

When the noose slips around his neck, its roughness chaffing the skin, a poor wretch knows he must be only moments away from meeting his maker. Yet a chosen few have enjoyed remarkable escapes.

One of the most celebrated cases was that of 'half-hanged Smith'. Yorkshire-born John Smith was a soldier, sailor and housebreaker. On 5 December 1705 he received the death sentence but immediately appealed. It appeared his efforts were in vain. On Christmas Eve he was taken by cart to Tyburn and his hanging commenced. He had been dangling by the neck for some five minutes when a horseman galloped to the scene trumpeting the news: 'A reprieve, a reprieve!'

Word spread among the crowd until it was a chant. Smith was cut down from the triple tree and taken to a nearby house where he was revived. When he was suitably recovered he told how he felt great pain as the hanging began. His spirits, he said, were in a 'strange commotion, violently pressing upwards'. After that he saw a blaze of light before losing all sensation. It was only after he was cut down that he began to experience the agonies of strangulation once more.

Sadly, the narrow escape did not reform 'half-hanged' Smith although his luck did not desert him. When he found himself before an Old Bailey jury on a burglary charge they were sympathetic to his previous ordeal and did not punish him. A second time in the same courtroom, Smith learned that the prosecutor had died the day before his trial. It is not known if Smith survived or was hanged again.

**WHEN THE NOOSE SLIPS AROUND HIS NECK, ITS ROUGHNESS CHAFFING THE SKIN, A POOR WRETCH KNOWS HE MUST BE ONLY MOMENTS AWAY FROM MEETING HIS MAKER. YET A CHOSEN FEW HAVE ENJOYED REMARKABLE ESCAPES.**

## RISING FROM THE DEAD

Margaret Dickson, of Musselburgh, Scotland, appeared before the courts in 1728 accused of killing a new-born child, after being denounced by neighbours. While she admitted being unfaithful to her husband, who was away at sea, she firmly denied murdering an infant. Nevertheless, she was sentenced at Edinburgh to hang.

Even as the rope was around her neck she declared her innocence. The hanging went ahead and later she was cut down by friends, placed in a coffin and they set off back for Musselburgh. Two miles from the city the friends stopped for a drink at a village called Pepper Mill. As they were supping, one of them gasped in terror. The lid of the coffin was moving. Cautiously, they approached and gently slid off the coffin cover. Margaret Dickson sat bolt upright – as her pals scattered in fear.

She was put to bed at the inn but, by the following morning, was fit enough to walk to her house. Scottish law did not allow her to be hanged again. Her husband arrived home and married her once more, silencing the fishwives of Musselburgh.

## CARPENTER'S GALLOWS HUMOUR

Public hangman James Berry, in post between 1884 and 1892, was a conscientious man. He ensured the gallows he used were in pristine condition and were tested regularly.

It seemed like another routine hanging when he was called on to dispatch the Babbacombe murderer John Lee. When the preliminaries were over Berry guided Lee to stand on the platform doors. The convicted man's hands and feet were bound and the noose was placed around his neck. Swiftly, Berry moved to the side and pulled the lever to send Lee to his doom. Nothing happened.

Three times Lee was put in place and the lever was pulled. Three times it failed to work. Yet when the machinery was tested while the prisoner stood to one side, it worked perfectly. The ordeal for Lee lasted a full half-hour. Afterwards he was given a reprieve on account of the anguish he suffered.

One explanation emerged years later when a convict took credit for the failed hanging. As a carpenter, he claimed he was the one who put up the gallows, which were inside a jail, and that he managed to wedge the doors. He joined the inspection of the gallows and managed to hide the wedge but re-inserted it before the next attempt at hanging Lee.

# NOOSE

A prisoner is cut down from the gallows after a last minute reprieve.

# TYBURN – LONDON'S GALLOWS

## LONDON'S PRIMARY EXECUTION SITE WAS TYBURN

## WHICH STOOD BETWEEN WHAT IS NOW MARBLE ARCH

## AND THE WESTERN END OF OXFORD STREET.

**Above: Tyburn was a quiet country venue when there were no hangings.**

**Above, right: Another popular place of execution in London was Smithfield, the horse market.**

Given its bulging population, London conducted more executions than most of Europe's capital cities.

London's primary execution site was Tyburn which stood between what is now Marble Arch and the western end of Oxford Street. The Tyburn is a river with two branches running through West London. Along its banks were elm trees which were first used for hanging. A pair of gallows were first installed on the site in 1220. The Tyburn Tree came in 1571 and was used until 1759 when it was branded an obstruction to the highway. In fact, it was the mob scenes on hanging days that prompted the authorities to abandon the Tyburn Tree. Mobile gallows operated at the site until public executions ceased there in 1783.

## GRANDSTAND

So popular was Tyburn that it boasted its own grandstand. Scaffolding erected in 1724 offered vantage-point seats to the those that could afford them. It was known as Mother Procter's Pews. When Earl Ferrers was hanged in 1760 the takings at the Pews topped £5,000.

**AT THE LAST PUBLIC EXECUTION AT NEWGATE IN 1868 'A GREAT CRY ROSE FROM THE CROWD AS THE CULPRIT FELL'.**

## THE LAST EXECUTION AT TYBURN

*The Times* carried an account of the last public execution at Newgate in 1868, that of Michael Barrett, convicted of causing an explosion at Clerkenwell.

'...the mass of people was immense...Now and then there was great laughter as a girl fainted and was passed out hand over hand above the heads of the mob, and then there came a scuffle and a fight, and then a hymn, and then a sermon, and then a comic song and so on from hour to hour...

'With the first sound of the bells came a great hungry roar from the crowd outside and a loud, continued shout of "Hats Off" till the whole dense bareheaded mass stood white and ghastly-looking in the morning sun, and the pressure on the barriers increased so that the girls and women in the front rank began to scream and struggle to get free.

'Barrett walked up coolly and boldly...There was a partial burst of cheers which was instantly accompanied by loud hisses and so it remained for some seconds till as the last moment approached the roars dwindled down to a dead silence...

'It is worthy of remark that a great cry rose from the crowd as the culprit fell – a cry which was neither an exclamation nor a scream but it partook of the sound of both. With the fall of the drop the crowd began to disperse, but an immense mass waited till the time for cutting down came...'

## JOINING THE PARADE

To the joy of the crowd, a hanging at Tyburn meant a veritable parade from the jail at Newgate which could last anything up to two hours, depending on the numbers jostling around the route. The first recorded hanging at Tyburn came in 1196 when William Fitzosbert was hanged for sedition. The last to die at Tyburn was John Austin on 7 November 1783. By then the procession to Tyburn was deemed an unsavoury display of barbarism by the authorities.

Writer Samuel Johnson echoed the disgust of many at this policy change when he said: 'The old method was most satisfactory to all parties; the public was gratified by a procession, the criminal is supported by it. Why is all this to be swept away?' Johnson felt, like many, that the greater the number who witnessed the execution, the greater its deterrent effect. The sheriff replied that the Tyburn procession was ended in the interests of justice. Thereafter executions took place upon a newly constructed gallows at Newgate.

In London alone there were other regular execution spots, including St Giles, Smithfield, Westminster, Knightsbridge, Islington and many others. Seafarers were hung at Execution Dock in Wapping at low tide. The bodies of those convicted of piracy, mutiny and so forth were then hung in chains on the muddy banks of the Thames for three tides to wash over them, by way of warning to other sailors who faced the grisly sight as they used the busy waterway.

Newspapers purporting to contain the last words of the condemned man were widely sold. Some conmen peddled the same facts for different men and few noticed the difference.

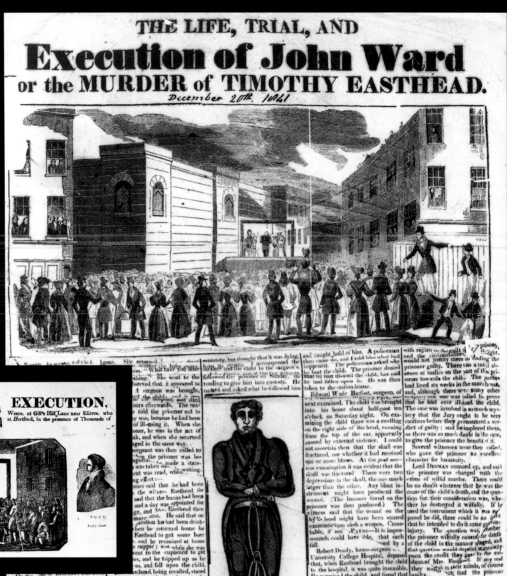

# AUDIENCE PARTICIPATION

The spectacle of death summoned eager audiences which numbered well into the thousands. People flocked to watch a poor fellow or wretched woman writhe in agony at the end of a rope.

If the felon was a folk hero, he was cheered on his way. If he was guilty of a vile crime he was booed, jeered and pelted with garbage, dung or dead animals. Far from weeping, the on-lookers were just as likely to break out in to song. 'Oh my, think I've got to die!' was a popular choice.

Execution days were a public holiday. Mothers took their children to teach them a lesson for life – and flogged them afterwards to ensure the message hit home. Hawkers joined the throng to sell their wares, including food and drink for the spectators.

> 'A COMELY-LOOKING MAN HE WAS AND KEPT HIS COUNTENANCE TO THE END; I WAS SORRY TO SEE HIM.'
> – SAMUEL PEPYS ON COLONEL TURNER, HANGED FOR ROBBERY.

## FAMOUS LAST WORDS

On sale too were sheets of paper purporting to contain the last words written by the condemned man or woman. There was an artist's impression, perhaps, and a poem. There was, of course, nothing to test the accuracy of the printed word and some sheets appeared to be repetitions of previous ones. Ordinaries, the suspect clergymen who attended the condemned in their final days, made a fine living from writing such broadsheets.

Pickpockets had a field day, perhaps stealing far more than the convict being hanged had ever done. Many in the crowd would have been drunk. After 1720 the nation's favourite tipple was gin which was cheaply produced. By 1750 there was allegedly one gin shop in London for every 120 citizens.

Loud, lewd and sometimes riotous, there was little surrounding an execution scene that offered solace to the condemned and precious few signs of respect for their plight.

Hangings occurred in towns and cities all over Britain and Ireland in the 18th century. Sometimes a regular venue was used, at other times the hanging was carried out at the scene of the crime. Many provinces retained the services of an executioner. When the number of hangings diminished in the later years of the century, and transport systems improved, it became common practice to request the services of an executioner from out of town.

## SAMUEL PEPYS

Sometimes gallows were placed as close as possible to the scenes of the crime. Diarist Samuel Pepys (above) saw a criminal called Colonel Turner hanged at Leadenhall Street where the convicted man had committed robbery. 'And there I got for a shilling to stand upon the wheel of a cart, in great pain, above an hour before the execution was done; he delaying the time by long discourses and prayers, one after another in hopes of a reprieve; but none came, and at last he was flung off the ladder in his cloak. A comely-looking man he was and kept his countenance to the end; I was sorry to see him. It was believed there were at least 12,000 to 14,000 people in the street.'

# THE BODY

In the pursuit of knowledge, surgeons down the centuries have required one basic tool of the trade – a dead body. Yet corpses were surprisingly tricky to come by.

Even today, when society has been stripped of its superstitions regarding death, comparatively few will leave their bodies to science. In days gone by the fears of having their lifeless bodies prodded and probed by surgeons gripped folk, who cared little for the progress of medicine. It was to them the ultimate humiliation and might even impede their entry into the afterlife

The Royal College of Physicians in London was allowed, by Royal assent, to have the bodies of six men from the gallows each year. The Company of Barber-Surgeons were permitted the corpses of four more. All dissections were carried out publicly.

# SNATCHERS

## BLACK MARKET IN BODIES

But that small number could not satisfy the medics of the 16th and 17th centuries when there was still so much to discover. In addition there were private surgeons equally driven to find out about anatomy and eager to get to work on any dead body they could.

Surgeons were sometimes charged huge amounts for bodies. In 1694 the Royal College paid 35 shillings (£1.75) to obtain and ship back a body from Tyburn. Between 1715 and 1750 the Company of Barber-Surgeons spent a total of £465 on obtaining the corpses to which it was entitled.

That led, of course, to an illicit trade in the bodies of the condemned. The hangman would covertly supplement his wages by selling off those he cut down from the gallows. There was an army of shady body snatchers at work for the relatively easy money available. Knowing via public hangings who was recently buried, the condemned were always their favoured prey.

## CLAIMING THE CORPSES

There were enormous problems facing agents of surgeons attending a gallows. It was even difficult to get the corpses they were entitled to. Ranged against them were the family and friends of the condemned, or comrades. Notoriously quick to claim the corpses were the Irish and sailors.

Families found new, strong bonds when the doomsday loomed. Fathers, husbands, wives and siblings would travel for miles to claim a corpse and give it a decent burial. Some would even employ a surgeon to stand by at a nearby house in the hope the executed man or woman could be revived. The patriotic Irish were even more fervent in the protection of their countrymen while sailors held an enmity towards surgeons, mainly due to the high death rate at sea. The matelot nickname for surgeons in the 18th century was 'crocus', a play on the phrase 'croak us' meaning to kill.

The net result were minor riots at Tyburn and at Execution Dock in Wapping as representatives of the surgeons and the cohorts of the dead men tussled over the body.

After a variety of pleas from the medical profession, the law stepped in with the 'Murder Act' of 1752 which stated 'it has become necessary that some further terror and peculiar mark of infamy be added to the punishment.' Now all those hung whether it be for murder or on some other charge would be taken afterwards to the surgeons who would complete the punishment. Families and friends would still battle to retrieve the corpse but they had the full weight of the law against them now. The price of corpses plummeted and the days of the body snatchers were over.

**The terror of being publicly dissected haunted people in the 17th century. Family and friends would go to any lengths to reclaim the body of a hanged man and cheat the surgeons.**

## DICK TURPIN

Infamous highwayman Dick Turpin nearly landed up in the hands of the surgeons. Although friends made his grave in St George's churchyard, York, deeper than usual it did not deter body snatchers. But the nightworkers were spotted and friends of Turpin went into action, finding the missing corpse in a surgeon's garden. The body was then laid on a board, paraded through the streets back to the churchyard and covered in caustic lime before being buried once more.

## SELLING BODIES

A few men chose to sell their own condemned bodies before the execution took place. In the middle of the 18th century veteran soldier John Fontenoy asked a surgeon to buy his body so he could meet his prison expenses. In 1752 William Signal sold his own body to buy decent clothes in which to hang.

## ANGEL OF MERCY

Seventeen-year-old William Duell was hung at Tyburn in 1740 for half an hour before being taken to the slab at Surgeon's Hall. Just as they were about to cut him open they heard him groan. He was alive, just. With the help of the surgeons – who had moments before been preparing to cut him open – he recovered. He told them he had been in paradise where an angel said his sins were forgiven. Having survived, he was not sentenced to hang again but transported for life instead.

# PUNISHING THE DEAD

**AFTER HANGING, THE DEAD BODIES OF MEN GUILTY OF COLD-BLOODED CRIMES WOULD BE SUSPENDED IN CHAINS BY WAY OF WARNING TO OTHERS.**

The death penalty was not harsh enough for some of the law-makers of previous centuries. After all, the rising rate of crime proved that public hangings were doing little to deter the populace. A stronger punishment was needed to terrorise them into good behaviour.

With this in mind, the government alighted on a further punishment which would strike a chord with the masses. After hanging, the dead bodies of men guilty of cold-blooded crimes would be suspended in chains by way of warning to others tempted by a life of crime. It became the fate of numerous highwaymen.

There are instances of notorious criminals being hung in chains throughout the 16th and 17th centuries. But it was the Murder Act of 1752 which included the notion of hanging in chains either after, or instead of, dissection. The sight of a swinging body on a gibbet prominently placed at a crossroads or at the scene of a crime thereafter became commonplace.

## THEM DRY BONES

Lord Justice Clerk used these chilling words when he pronounced sentence on Alexander Gillam at Inverness in 1810. 'I have therefore determined that after your execution you shall be hung in chains until the fowls of the air pick the flesh off your body and your bones bleach and whiten in the winds of heaven, thereby to afford a constant warning of the fatal consequences which almost invariably attend the indulgence of the passions.'

The body of butcher John Breed who killed neighbour Thomas Lamb in 1742 was displayed on a gibbet for years, until all but the upper part of the skull had fallen off and disappeared.

In 1747 on England's northern border the body of murderer Adam Graham was hung on a gibbet 12 yards high and studded with 12,000 nails to prevent a rescue bid by friends or family.

In a bid to prolong the 'life' of the gibbet corpse it was frequently tarred. The bodies of three highwaymen were blackened and gibbeted near Belper, Derbyshire, in the 1750s. Within a few weeks a concerned comrade of the dead men torched the gibbet, sparing the trio an endless indignity by cremating the bodies until they were ashes.

## HANGED, DRAWN AND QUARTERED

In Western Europe – until as recently as the 18th century – convicted traitors were hanged, drawn and quartered. The prisoner was 'drawn' to the place of execution on hurdles, hanged until almost dead and then disembowled. All this was carried out with the victim alive and often concious. The finale to this brutal punishment was the quartering, whereby the body was divided into four quarters.

**Left: The dangling bodies of dead men – some caged to prevent a rescue attempt – were like eerie spectres around the countryside.**

## SWINGING IN THE WIND

The corpse creaking in the wind was an affecting sight. Travellers would take detours which added miles and hours to their journey in order to avoid the lurid spectacle on a lonely road. Yet mobs were often found baying and hooting at the foot of an urban gibbet. London was said to be deserted one summer's day in 1795 after the population went en masse to Wimbledon where three bodies were gibbeted.

The last killer to be hung in chains was in Leicester in 1834. Later the same year the practice was outlawed in Britain. Gibbeting was also common in Europe. Most notable of the French gibbets was the one at Montfaucon with space enough for more than 500 offenders.

## CHAINED ALIVE

Sometimes a felon was hung in chains while he was still alive so that he died of hunger, thirst or exposure. A compassionate traveller happening upon the wretch might put an end to the misery, by running him through with a sword. This savage penalty was rarely employed and had all but died out in Europe by the 18th century.

However, highwayman John Whitfield was so detested in the community where he was captured that he was hung alive in chains at Durham in 1777 and left to perish. It was several days before a mailcoach man dispatched him with a single shot.

# HEALING TOUCH OF THE EXECUTED

**WITH VIOLENT DEATH CAME HOPE FOR THE LIVING AS THE CORPSE WAS HELD TO HAVE MAGIC HEALING POWERS.**

As the hanged man expired, hordes of people pressed forward hoping to brush with his body. The executioner assisted (above left) by severing the hand to sell to someone in the crowd.

Some people watched public executions because they enjoyed the spectacle. Others went for the benefit of their health.

In Norfolk, it was believed that a brush with a hanged man's hand cured conditions such as goitre and tumours. In Wessex the same treatment was prescribed for ulcers and cancers. As the corpse's hand rotted, so the lump or ailment was said to diminish. In Somerset any swelling was thought to be cured at the touch of a dead man who had been publicly hanged.

The old wives of Dorset swore touching a condemned man's newly dead body would alleviate skin complaints. It was widely held that a withered limb would be made whole and perfect again if it were laid against the neck of a recently hanged man.

In Herefordshire the touch of a rope that had been used on the gallows apparently saw off headaches. The same remedy in Lincolnshire, allegedly, cured fits. Further north the population would seek splinters taken from the gallows to cure toothache. Braver souls would actually bite the teeth from the mouth of an executed man, in order to guard against the same affliction.

## MAGIC HANDS

Nurses brought children to the foot of the gibbet to stroke the hand of the dead. This was done in the sure and certain belief that the youngsters would enjoy lifelong good health. Barren women came, too, in the hope that the 'magic' hand of the dead would enable them to conceive. Those cursed with a fever would happily don a bag around their neck containing wood chippings from the gallows, thinking that it would cure them. The 'death sweat' of a man on the gallows was a remedy for tuberculosis.

In 1789 a Frenchman travelling around Britain was astonished to see a beautiful young woman, in the grip of the executioner, publicly bare her breasts so that the hands of the hanged man could be placed upon them.

This unsavoury act was probably carried out in order to treat an unknown affliction.

It wasn't only the lower orders of society who believed in the powers emanating from corpses. A well-appointed young woman was seen to approach the dangling body of Dr Dodd, hanged in 1777, and place his cooling hands on a tumour that blighted her face.

After one hanging at Tyburn a wealthy woman holding a three-year-old child in her arms made her way to the gallows. Gently she passed the hand of the dead man three times over the child's infected hand.

## THE LUCKY ROPE

In 1818 a hangman was reported to be charging those in the crowd two shillings and sixpence (12½p) to touch the corpse. Likewise, the hangman's rope was also in demand. Many believed that if they owned a piece of rope which had once strangled someone they would never themselves be hanged. It was lucky for gamblers to have the rope and, if it was wound around the temples, it was said to end headaches.

Great credence appears to have been given to these superstitions during the 18th century. Much of the folklore was laid to rest, however, with the decline in public executions in the 19th century.

## THE 'HAND OF GLORY'

Burglars coveted a 'hand of glory', the hand of a hanged man which had been dried, pickled and turned into a candle-holder. Instead of using candles, the fingers were sometimes set on fire. They believed that when they entered a house bearing this gruesome charm the occupants would fall under a spell and allow the intruders to carry out their unlawful work in peace.

## ROBBING THE GIBBET

When corpses were gibbeted there was ample opportunity for people to pursue their morbid superstitions. Some removed skulls to use as cups for those suffering from epilepsy. Moss scraped from the surface of a long-exposed skull was used as snuff to cure headaches.

# RUTH ELLIS

The last woman to hang in Britain was Ruth Ellis. She shot her boyfriend David Blakely with a Smith and Wesson revolver after he emerged from a pub in Hampstead on Easter Sunday, 1955. She was guilty of pre-meditated murder – but did she deserve to die? The story behind the killing did much to aid the abolitionist cause in Britain.

Ruth Ellis (nee Neilson) was born in Wales, one of five children. When she was still a child her father changed his career and moved to London as a chauffeur.

After having a war baby by a French-Canadian soldier, lone mother Ruth settled on a career in clubland working as a hostess. It was

**RUTH ELLIS FIRED A SMITH AND WESSON GUN AND KILLED THE MAN SHE LOVED, JUST TWO WEEKS AFTER SHE'D HAD A MISCARRIAGE.**

her job to get the punters to part with their cash. A shapely blonde, she slept with men for money and for fun.

Eventually she married an alcoholic dentist, George Ellis. The relationship was stormy mostly because Ruth was consumed by an irrational jealousy. Their problems became too great and, despite the birth of a daughter, George Ellis fled the marriage.

Ruth, 27, met the fresh-faced David Blakely, three years her junior, across the bar after she returned to work following the break-up of her marriage. Their relationship, like her marriage, became hallmarked by Ruth's suspicious wrath. David was another heavy drinker and was also capable of violence and cruelty.

The relationship went on a downward spiral of accusation and counter-accusation, of attack and counter-attack. Blakely was physically and mentally exhausted by Ruth and took a sexual stimulant in order to keep up with her demands in bed. When David made convincing attempts to break off this mutually damaging courtship Ruth obtained a gun and shot him.

It was a cold-blooded killing and the jury took just 14 minutes to reach a verdict of guilty to murder. Yet it happened less than two weeks after Ruth suffered a miscarriage brought about by Blakely's violence. Afterwards, she saw Blakely flirting with another woman and was inflamed by jealousy, unhinging her reason.

As she was sentenced to death Ruth Ellis managed a smile for her family and friends sitting in the public gallery. But in prison the veneer cracked. All attempts to commute the death sentence failed and at least once Ruth threw herself on her cell bed screaming 'I don't want to die'.

She regained her composure knowing that her every move was widely reported outside prison. On 13 July 1955 she sipped a warm brandy before walking to the execution shed at Holloway prison.

**Left: Crowds gathered outside Holloway jail in London as Ruth Ellis (right) prepared to hang inside. Although platinum blonde Ellis was guilty of cold-blooded murder many considered that she had been driven to distraction and deserved compassion.**

## PUBLIC FEELING

William Connor, writing under the pen name Cassandra in the *Daily Mirror*, reflected the arguments of the abolitionists. 'Ruth Ellis does not matter any more than her two most recent female predecessors to the hangman's noose – Mrs Merrifield and Mrs Christofi. 'But what we do to her – you and I – matters very much, and if we continue to do it to her sad successors then we all bear the guilt of savagery untinged with mercy.'

# THE ELECTRIC

The electric chair was first used on 6 August 1890 in Auburn prison, New York. It was very nearly the last time it was used, too, for witnesses were horrified by its effect.

In the chair was a wife-killer named William Kemmler, of Buffalo, New York. In court his attorney had been paid for by the Westinghouse (Alternating Current) Electricity Company which was fearful that electricity would suddenly be considered dangerous by users with the advent of the chair. It was to no avail and Kemmler was found guilty.

He sat passively in the wooden hot seat as a metal cap containing an electrode was fitted to his head and a second electrode was attached to his back. When the electrical current was switched on it seriously singed his flesh. But when the charge of 1,300 volts was ended after 17 seconds Kemmler still breathed. Another shock lasting 70 seconds finally ended his life. The scene and the smell were nauseating to the assembled crowd who were equally concerned that Kemmler had taken so long to die.

## BREAKDOWN OF CHAIR

Worse was to follow. On 27 July 1893 William Taylor was in the chair at Auburn when its back snapped during the first charge. Hastily, the unconscious Taylor was removed to another room and given chloroform and morphine injections to ensure he was not revived. When the chair was fixed – one hour and ten minutes later – he was put in it once more and the execution was completed. There are other stories of six-inch flames shooting out when the current is switched on.

Yet the authorities in New York were not deterred. By 1906 more

# CHAIR

than 100 murderers had been dispatched in the electric chairs housed in Auburn jail, Dannemora jail and Sing Sing. After 1914 all the state's electric chair executions were carried out at Sing Sing.

Other states adopted the method, convinced it was in fact a quick and humane route to death. Thankfully, techniques and technology improved over the years to stop disasters happening.

## HOW THE CHAIR OPERATES

The electric chair, also known as 'Sparky', 'Old Smokey' and the 'Hot Squat', is still made of wood – usually oak. On it are straps to secure the arms, legs, head and chest of the victims. In preparation the victims are shaved both on their heads and their right legs, where the electrodes, moistened with saline solution, are fitted.

From behind the executioner operates the chair. The first shock is at around 2,000 volts. It is followed by two lesser charges and then again by another mighty blast. Death should occur immediately because the body is paralysed and the brain destroyed by the initial shock. Critics of the chair claim that death is not always instant. One victim needed five charges of electricity and 17 minutes in the chair before he was pronounced dead.

Dozens of select witnesses watch these executions. Sheriffs, journalists, relations of the convicted man and the family of the criminal's victims are all present.

## EYE-WITNESS ACCOUNT

Reporter Mike James describes the execution of 26-year-old rapist Ray Anderson on 9 June 1939:

'Out of consideration for the executioner, the room in which he pulls the switch is usually separated from the chair by a wall or partition. This is supposed to make the puller of the death lever feel more clinical and impersonal about it – less guilty.

'The warden raised his hand. The executioner in the next room closed the circuit. There was a hum like a diesel train getting underway; an unreal bluish light filled the room. The man in the chair rose as if to get up quickly and run out, but he was stopped abruptly, joltingly in mid-air by the restraining straps. His body, straining against the straps, seemed about to burst them and take flight. His hair sparked and sizzled with bluish flame for an instant. Then the humming sound stopped; 2200 volts dropped out from under him and he slumped back into the chair, no longer a man but a body.'

## SURVIVING THE SHOCK

In 1946 the unthinkable happened when 17-year old Willie Francis (above) survived the electric chair. A witness reported: 'I heard the one in charge yell to the man outside for more juice when he saw that Willie Francis was not dying, and the one on the outside yelled back he was giving him all he had. Then Willie Francis cried out: 'Take it off. Let me breathe.'

Afterwards Francis said: 'I felt a burning in my head and my left leg and I jumped against the straps. I saw little blue and pink and green speckles.' Despite his ordeal Francis failed to win a pardon and was executed a year later.

# THE GAS CHAMBER

**Pigs were the first victims of the gas chamber. After watching their suffering journalists were appalled.**

Like the electric chair, the gas chamber was another invention hailed as humane, but which earned a blasting from the critics.

It was first introduced in Nevada in 1924, to a lukewarm reception. When one was installed in San Quentin Prison in the early 1930s local newspapers were at first enthusiastic. But when reporters attended an experimental gassing of pigs they were repulsed. One said it was more barbaric than being hanged, drawn and quartered! In 1938 newspapers were once again critical of the gas chamber after two convicted murderers took 15 minutes to die.

The gas chamber is a sealed room containing a chair which is bolted to the floor. Prisoners are strapped to the chair and a stethoscope is attached to their chests. Listening in on the other end of the stethoscope, which leads outside the chamber, is a doctor who can monitor the progress of the execution.

## WHEN IT WAS FIRST INTRODUCED THE GAS CHAMBER WAS LABELLED HUMANE. BUT TWO CONVICTED KILLERS TOOK 15 MINUTES TO DIE.

## DON'T HOLD YOUR BREATH

When the door is firmly shut a deadly cyanide gas is released into the chamber which poisons the prisoners when they inhale. Ironically, the process will take longer if the prisoners hold their breath and fight for a few seconds more of life. The gasping and spluttering of the victims is undoubtedly distressing for witnesses.

Once a prisoner is dead, a fan expels the poisoned air from inside the chamber through a tall chimney.

## CONVULSING AND GASPING FOR AIR AS THE POISON GAS SEEPS IN ONLY PROLONGS THE AGONY FOR GAS CHAMBER VICTIMS.

## STOP-STOP-GO EXECUTION

Barbara Graham was the third woman ever to die at the behest of the Californian legal system. Mother-of-three Babs took part in the violent killing of Mabel Monahan. Graham and her three male accomplices attacked Mrs Monahan in her home convinced there was a stash of money in the house belonging to a gambling baron to whom she was related. The court heard that Graham had pistol-whipped Mrs Monahan as she lay helpless on the floor.

Graham was scheduled to die in the gas chamber of San Quentin on 3 June 1955 after spending two years on Death Row. She arrived from the Corona women's prison at 4 pm the previous day, weak with fear and suffering from nagging toothache. She refused a last meal. 'Why waste good food on me?' she asked the warden acidly. 'Give it to someone who can enjoy it.'

Outside the walls of the jail Graham's legal team were working in earnest and, in the early hours of the morning, won a stay of execution. Inside, Graham awoke, showered, put on make-up, did her hair and donned a smart beige suit not hearing until 9.20 am that a delay in the execution had been granted. Just

an hour later news arrived at the jail that the petitions filed for Graham had been denied.

At 10.44 Graham began the journey to the gas chamber and reached its door when word of another stay came through. She turned her back on the gas chamber and sobbed to the clergyman with her: 'Perhaps they've found out that I'm innocent?'

At 11.10 all hope was gone. The petition had once again been denied and now nothing would stand in the way of the execution. 'Why do they torture me so? I was ready to die at 10 o'clock,' wept Graham.

Twenty minutes afterwards she was led to the chamber and strapped in the chair. She requested a blindfold to avoid the gaze of witnesses and newsmen. During her final moments her lips moved in prayer as the poisonous fumes began to fill the chamber.

At first it seemed that she had died quickly and peacefully. But Graham had deceived the on-lookers – she had been holding her breath. Her head suddenly jerked up as she fended off the cyanide until her lungs could stand no more. She was forced to take a gulp of the poisoned air and died at 11.42 am.

# DEATH ROW

**CONDEMNED PRISONERS ARE USUALLY TAKEN OUT OF THE PRISON POPULATION TO LIVE OUT THE REST OF THEIR DAYS ON 'DEATH ROW'.**

Condemned prisoners are usually taken out of the general prison population to live out the rest of their days on 'death row'. With the appeals system taking ever longer, their fate can hang in the balance for years. In Indonesia one man, Mohammed Munir, was shot on the order of the courts more than 17 years after his arrest and trial for involvement in an attempted coup.

Some prisoners become obsessed by impending doom and are driven insane. Others put their time to good use and educate themselves by reading great works of literature or studying religion. The irony of this is that completely reformed characters, who bear no resemblance to the monsters who killed or maimed, are often executed.

## ADVANCE DEATH CERTIFICATES

In Florida condemned men are issued with a death warrant four weeks before they are due to be executed. They are then moved to cells in close proximity to the gas chamber or the electric chair. Four days before the execution the prisoner comes under round-the-clock guard and all personal items are removed. A death certificate is prepared in advance, giving cause of death as 'legal execution by . . .'. On the morning of the execution a last meal is served at 4.30 am. Then the prisoner's head and right leg is shaved for the execution to take place at 7 am.

A stay of execution can be issued at any time. This means it is not unusual for prisoners to endure the preparations for their execution several times.

**Above left: Death Row in Ohio State Penitentiary in 1958. The surroundings reflect the mood of the inmates who know how they are to die but have no idea when.**

**Left: Convicted prisoners seek solace as their future hangs in the balance.**

**Top: In clinical surroundings, Ohio's electric chair awaits its next victim. It is considered quick and clean, but victims may still take many minutes to die.**

## BAKED APPEL

**WHEN GANGSTER GEORGE APPEL WAS BEING STRAPPED INTO THE ELECTRIC CHAIR HE QUIPPED WITH WATCHING NEWSMEN: 'WELL FOLKS, YOU'LL SOON SEE A BAKED APPEL'.**

## LAST-MINUTE REPRIEVES OVERTURNED

British-born Nicholas Ingram was due to be executed by electric chair at 7 pm on Thursday, 6 April 1995 in Georgia. With just an hour to spare his lawyers won a 24 hour stay of execution. He wrote afterwards: 'Apparently at 5.55 pm my case was stayed, but nobody told me – they began seriously to prepare me for execution. It was devoid of humanity, a bunch of sick people who apparently volunteered for the job, acting like I was an animal, a sheep being prepared for slaughter. They shaved my head with electric shears then used a razor to cut it shorter and to shave my right shin.'

The next day Ingram won a 72-hour stay of execution but it was challenged by the district attorney. At 6 pm the court overturned the stay and the procedures of execution began all over again. Ingram died at 9 pm.

Other condemned prisoners may be close enough to hear the whirring sound of the electric chair as it goes into action. They will maintain an all-night vigil if one of their number is due to die, singing hymns out of respect. From their cells they may be able to see the condemned man make his final walk. Sometimes they see his coffin, too.

# DEATH-CELL LAWYER

The Red Light Bandit spread terror in Hollywood during January 1948. He preyed on courting couples, brandishing a gun, the fiend robbed the men and then sexually abused the women. On one occasion, two women were driven off to an isolated spot before their ordeals began.

After Caryl Whittier Chessman, 26, was arrested the police were confident they had fingered the attacker. In the subsequent court case Chessman was identified by his victims. On 21 May 1948 he was found guilty on 17 charges and for the kidnappings and assaults he was given the death penalty.

On 25 June 1948 Judge Charles Fricke, by a quirk of law, sentenced Chessman to die not once – but twice – in the gas chamber of San Quentin. In addition a life imprisonment without parole was handed down to Chessman,

## CHESSMAN FIRED OFF A VOLLEY OF APPEALS, CASTING ABOUT FOR THE LEGAL LOOPHOLE THAT WOULD SAVE HIM.

eight consecutive five-years-to-life terms and four lesser sentences.

Chessman was taken to Death Row at San Quentin from where he proved he was no ordinary prisoner. He had already been incarcerated at San Quentin for a series of armed robberies and, during his time behind bars, became something of an academic. He had been released on parole in December 1947.

Now Chessman – who denied to the end that he was the Red Light Bandit – was going to stretch his philosophical skills to the limit in a bid to have the capital sentence quashed. Working feverishly at a typewriter, Chessman fired off a volley of appeals, desperately casting about for the legal loophole that would save him. He pored over legal text books, scrutinising each section and sub section of the law. Each time he thought he had tri-- umphed he was knocked back by the courts and another date for his execution was set.

## PAINFUL SIGN

Reporter Will Stevens, who was a witness at the execution, had agreed a signal with the condemned man. Chessman was to give it if he was in agony. Five minutes after execution began, Chessman made the signal.

## IN THE SHADOW OF DEATH

As numerous appeals were being lodged on Chessman's behalf, he wrote: 'Behind me were more than six years, six eternities, of living in the shadow of the gas chamber, of fighting a dogged and seemingly endless battle for survival, of watching nearly five dozen men take that last grim walk past my cell. It had been an incredible, nightmarish experience, and during the first four years of it I hadn't given a damn whether I lived or died. I'd been interested only in cheating the executioner and in seeing that Death Row didn't break me, didn't whip me. It hadn't.

'Out of the experience had come an ultimate awakening and an overriding determination to give some affirmative meaning to an existence shaped, controlled and directed by psychopathic bondage and crime.'

## BEST-SELLING AUTHOR

**Caryl Chessman was a thoroughly reformed character before he died in the gas chamber at San Quentin.**

In 1954 Chessman saw his first book published. *Cell 2455, Death Row* was acclaimed by psychologists everywhere as a remarkable insight into the criminal mind. But Chessman was arguably no longer a criminal. With his writing came a transformation in character. He now rejected the wild days of his youth and embraced a new beginning.

He had a second book under way and appealed for his execution date, 14 May 1954, to be set aside so he could complete it. His application was refused.

The sentence was ultimately stayed once more as a new defence attorney took on Chessman's case.

In fact, he endured the torture of death row for a dozen years. But time ran out for Caryl Chessman on the morning of 2 May 1960. From his tiny cell he heard on the radio that the Supreme Court had turned down his application for a stay. It was broadcast 45 minutes before he was due to enter the gas chamber.

Lawyers were still making frantic efforts on his behalf. But Chessman became resigned to his fate. He entered the gas chamber moments after 10 am after smoking a final cigarette. As he was being strapped into the chair in the gas chamber, Chessman twice declared: 'I'm all right.'

Just as the cyanide pellets were being released and Chessman began fighting for breath there was a hubbub. A phone message had come through telling of a last-minute reprieve. However, the warden decided the proceedings had gone too far and could not be stopped. The execution continued and Chessman was gassed.

Could the state executioner have saved Chessman by switching on the powerful fans to rid the chamber of the poison gas? Should he have donned a gas mask at the scene and burst into the chamber? Nobody can say whether Chessman might still be alive today if the warden had made a different decision.

# EXECUTION BY FIRING SQUAD

The advent of guns in the 15th century did not bring about firing squads. Early firearms were far too inaccurate to ensure death. But, despite its slow start, this method of execution became the most popular form of capital punishment in the 20th century. In 1989 no fewer than 86 countries carried out capital punishments by firing squad. Only 78 countries used hanging although many sanctioned the use of both.

In 1970 Thailand appointed just one man, Pathom Kruapeng, to be the country's 'firing squad'. Each shooting was accompanied by ritual as Pathom, a practising Bhuddist, asked the victim for forgiveness by raising a stone and a yellow flower to the sky.

The victim was strapped in a chair positioned behind a cloth screen, his arms were outstretched and tied onto a long pole. In one hand were scented joss sticks and in the other, flowers.

Pathom, unaware of the identity of his victim, fired an automatic rifle through the screen at his target. He continued to fire until an observer raised a red flag, indicating the prisoner was dead.

The margin for error is not reduced when a number of guns are used. Often the squad members are instructed to aim at the trunk of the body because it is easier to hit than the head. This means the prisoner can take many minutes to die from the mortal wounds inflicted upon him. To alleviate feelings of guilt, sometimes members of the firing squad are issued with blanks so no one knows who fired the fatal shot.

To the south of the Tyburn gallows was the spot where military executions were carried out in London. Mutineers and other offenders in the army were lined up and shot in Hyde Park at what is now Speaker's Corner.

In Britain during the First World War all those sentenced to death for espionage bar one were executed by firing squad in the confines of the Tower of London. A squad of eight carried out the sentence with their victim bound and blindfolded in a chair.

In 1953 a report by a British Royal Commission into capital punishment rejected firing squads outright. 'It does not possess even the first requisite of an efficient method, the certainty of causing immediate death,' the report read.

## LETHAL INJECTION

Death by injection is unique to the United States where up to 19 states employ it against capital offenders. It was first introduced in 1977 in the states of Oklahoma and Texas. The first prisoner to die from it was Charles Brooks of Texas, in December 1982.

A combination of drugs are given intravenously. Although the exact measures may vary, the aim is to make the prisoner immediately unconscious, to then paralyse his muscles and to bring about heart failure.

Difficulties in administering this method of death come if the victim has been a long-term drug user and has deeply scarred veins. Sometimes minor surgery is required to insert the needle.

If the prisoner struggles then the cocktail of drugs might find its way into a muscle or other tissue, causing great pain. There is also a danger that the deadly substance may bind and block the tubes taking it into the body, prolonging death considerably. On 14 March 1984 James Autry met his end by lethal injection. A witness for *Newsweek* magazine reported that Autry took at least ten minutes to die, was conscious for much of the time and struggled, moaning in pain.

**Left: A firing squad goes into action in Mexico City in 1927.**

**Below: Whampoa pirates prepare for execution by firing squad at Kowloon in 1891.**

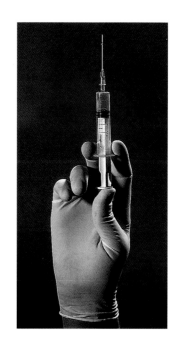

ROMANIAN TYRANT NICOLAE CEAUSESCU AND HIS WIFE ELENA WERE SHOT BY MACHINE GUN ON CHRISTMAS DAY 1989 FOLLOWING 22 YEARS OF AUTOCRATIC RULE AFTER A MILITARY COURT FOUND THEM GUILTY OF CRIMES AGAINST ROMANIA'S PEOPLE.

**Right: In the condemned cell at Newgate jail a doomed man seeks forgiveness and comfort from a clergyman. Many left the cell with the hope that a reprieve would yet save them.**

# AN EYE FOR AN EYE?

In favour of the death penalty are those who believe in retribution – 'an eye for an eye'. The Biblical quotation, they claim, paves the way for governments to take the life of someone who has killed. In addition, capital punishment protects society by preventing a felon from repeating his crime and provides a stark deterrent to the rest of society. Abolitionists have a different point of view.

Those opposed to capital punishment regard it as cold-blooded murder. The fact that it is carried out by government makes it no better than any other killing. Few authorities will admit to torturing prisoners. The unacceptable cruelty of torture has been internationally recognised and it is now regarded as shameful practice. Yet there are scores of governments which openly support hanging, shooting or electrocuting convicted criminals. The knowledge of impending death in the hands of the authorities must surely be the most acute torture available for prisoners.

The right to life is a basic human right. Does a murderer forgo that right after killing? Some would say yes, that he or she deserves to die. However, Amnesty International points out that human rights are not a reward for good behaviour and cannot be withdrawn for bad behaviour. They are for everybody. The poor, ethnic minorities and the politically controversial are the first to find their rights eroded and are in the majority on death row.

## THE DETERRENT EFFECT

There have been a variety of studies carried out to determine whether the death penalty is indeed a deterrent. None has been conclusive. It is true, however, that where the death penalty exists there is no significantly lower crime rate. Indeed, some research has pointed to a jump in the crime rate just after an execution. Criminals are deterred by the probability of detection rather than the severity of the punishment they will receive if caught.

## FATAL MISCARRIAGES

Where the death penalty exists a miscarriage of justice brings terrible consequences. Death is irreversible and all legal systems are fallible. It is inevitable that a proportion of all executed people are innocent.

The death penalty also creates martyrs. For those committing politically motivated crimes, an execution can bring valuable publicity and public symapthy for their cause.

Some killers deserve our compassion. Others become reformed characters after their convictions. And most compelling of all arguments against capital punishment – what if the person executed has committed no crime?

## THE DEATH PENALTY

**US** – The death penalty exists in some states. It is carried out by electrocution, lethal injection, lethal gas, hanging or shooting.

**France** – In 1981 the death penalty was finally abolished. An execution by guillotine was last carried out in 1977.

**Britain** – The Murder (Abolition of the Death Penalty) Act of 1965 abolished capital punishment for a five-year trial period. However before the period was up, it was made permanent in 1969.

**Australia** – The death penalty has been abolished state by state, starting with Queensland in 1922.

**Portugal** – Enlightened governments abolished the death penalty for political offences in 1852 and for criminal offences in 1867. The last execution of a common criminal was in April 1846.

**Saudi Arabia** – Death penalty is retained for a variety of offences. It is carried out by beheading or stoning.

**St Stephen was stoned to death – a punishment that is still carried out today. With their cruelty his killers made him a martyr and inadvertently helped his cause, Christianity.**

# INDEX

# PHOTOGRAPHIC ACKNOWLEDGEMENTS

Ancient Art and Architecture Collection 11, 22, 38 /39, 51, 52, 71 top, 97 bottom, 124 /125, 129 right, 130, 151; AKG London 2 /3 top, 2 top left, 8, 20 /21, 28 /29, 29 top, 70 /71, 83 bottom, 115 bottom, 142 /143, /Bibliothèque Nationale de France, Paris 143, /Henning Bock 18, /Erich Lessing /Musée Carnavalet 138 /139; Bridgeman Art Library /Bonhams, London 115 top, 39, 167, /Commonwealth Club, London 73 bottom, /Giraudon 2 bottom left, 122 /123, 126 /127, /Guildhall Library, Corporation of London 90 /91, 94 top, 110 left, /Houses of Parliament, Westminster, London 126, /Index 18 /19, /London Library, St James's Square, London 6, /Museum of London 186, /National Gallery of Scotland, Edinburgh 187, /O'Shea Gallery, London 86 /87, /Private Collection 54 /55, /Rafael Valls Gallery, London 159, 162, /Royal Geographical Society, London 3 bottom right, 66 /67, /R.S.A.F. Enfield Lock, Middlesex 174 top, /Victoria & Albert Museum, London 59, /The Trustees of the Weston Park Foundation 168; Calvert/Corbis 104 top; Corbis-Bettmann 33 top, 40, 94 bottom, 114, 118, 120, 120 /121, 137, 146 /147, 156 top, 176, 177, 178 /179, /UPI 6 /7, 80 top, 104 /105, 180 bottom, 180 top, 181, 183, 184 ; Mary Evans Picture Library 2 bottom right, 3 centre right, 4 /5, 14, 15 top, 15 bottom, 19, 26 /27, 30 31, 47, 52 /53, 56, 93, 98 /99, 108, 116 top, 116 bottom, 125, 160, 169; Hulton Getty Picture Collection 3 top right, 12, 12 /13, 16 top, 16 bottom, 17 bottom, 17 top, 24 /25, 25, 29 bottom, 30 right, 30 left, 32, 33 bottom, 34, 36, 37, 39, 44, 46 /47, 48 /49, 48, 49, 55, 58, 60 /61, 64, 68 bottom, 68 top, 69, 71 bottom, 72 /73, 72 bottom, 74 /75, 75, 76 /77, 77, 78, 80 bottom, 81, 87 bottom, 87 top, 88 /89, 88 bottom, 90 top left, 90 bottom, 92 /93, 94 /95, 97 top, 99, 100, 101 top, 101 bottom, 102 /103, 105, 110 /111, 110 right, 112 /113, 113 bottom, 113 top, 116 /117, 119, 124 bottom, 128, 129 left, 1310, 133, 134 /135, 135, 136 bottom, 136 top, 140 /141, 140, 144 bottom, 144 /145, 144 top, 146, 149, 150, 152, 152 /153, 154, 155, 156 bottom, 157, 158 /159, 160 /161, 161, 163, 164, 165, 166 main picture, 166 inset, 170, 171 left, 171 right, 172, 172 /173, 173 bottom, 174 bottom, 175, 182, 185 bottom; Images 10, 42 /43, 50, 62 /63, 63, 64 /65; Madame Tussaud's 148 /149, 148; Mansell Collection 3 bottom left, 22 /23, 26, 35, 40 /41, 60 bottom, 84 /85, 96, 102; National Library of Australia 79 left, 79 right; Popperfoto 83 top, 106 /107; Reed International Books Ltd 178; The Board of Trustees of the Royal Armouries 132; Science Photo Library /Saturn Stills 185 top; Topham Picturepoint 82 /83, 106.